Visual Insight
Flash 5 Keyboard Shortcuts

File Menu	Mac	PC
New	Cmd+N	Ctrl+N
Open	Cmd+O	Ctrl+O
Open as Library	Shift+Cmd+O	Shift+Ctrl+O
Close	Cmd+W	Ctrl+W
Save	Cmd+S	Ctrl+S
Save As	Shift+Cmd+S	Shift+Ctrl+S
Import	Cmd+R	Ctrl+R
Export Movie	Shift+Opt+Cmd+S	Shift+Alt+Ctrl+S
Publish Settings	Shift+Cmd+F12	Shift+Ctrl+F12
Publish	Shift+ F12	Shift +F12
Print	Cmd+P	Ctrl+P
Exit	Cmd+Q	Ctrl+Q

Edit Menu	Mac	PC
Undo	Cmd+Z	Ctrl+Z
Redo	Cmd+Y	Ctrl+Y
Cut	Cmd+X	Ctrl+X
Copy	Cmd+C	Ctrl+C
Paste	Cmd+V	Ctrl+V
Paste in Place	Shift+Cmd+V	Shift+Ctrl+V
Clear	Delete	Backspace
Duplicate	Cmd+D	Ctrl+D
Select All	Cmd+A	Ctrl+A
Deselect All	Shift+Cmd+A	Shift+Ctrl+A
Cut Frames	Opt+Cmd+X	Alt+Ctrl+X
Copy Frames	Opt+Cmd+C	Alt+Ctrl+C
Paste Frames	Opt+Cmd+V	Alt+Ctrl+V
Edit Symbols	Cmd+E	Ctrl+E

View Menu	Mac	PC
Zoom In	Cmd+=	Ctrl+=
Zoom Out	Cmd+-	Ctrl+-
Outlines	Opt+Shift+Cmd+0	Alt+Shift+Ctrl+0
Fast	Opt+Shift+Cmd+F	Alt+Shift+Ctrl+F
Antialias	Opt+Shift+Cmd+A	Alt+Shift+Ctrl+A
Antialias Text	Opt+Shift+Cmd+T	Alt+Shift+Ctrl+T
Timeline	Opt+ Cmd+T	Alt+ Ctrl+T
Work Area	Shift+Cmd+W	Shift+Ctrl+W
Rulers	Opt+Shift+Cmd+R	Alt+Shift+Ctrl+R
Snap to Objects	Shift+Cmd+/	Shift+Ctrl+/
Hide Edges	Cmd+H	Ctrl+H
Hide Panels	Tab	Tab

Insert Menu	Mac	PC
Convert to Symbol	F8	F8
New Symbol	Cmd+F8	Ctrl+F8
Frame	F5	F5
Remove Frames	Shift+F5	Shift+F5
Keyframe	F6	F6
Blank Keyframe	F7	F7
Clear Keyframe	Shift+F6	Shift+F6

Modify Menu	Mac	PC
Instance	Cmd+I	Ctrl+I
Frame	Cmd+F	Ctrl+F
Movie	Cmd+M	Ctrl+M
Optimize	Opt+Shift+Cmd+C	Alt+Shift+Ctrl+C
Group	Cmd+G	Ctrl+G
Ungroup	Shift+Cmd+G	Shift+Ctrl+G
Break Apart	Cmd+B	Ctrl+B

Text Menu	Mac	PC
Character	Cmd+T	Ctrl+T
Paragraph	Shift+Cmd+T	Shift+Ctrl+T

Control Menu	Mac	PC
Play	Return	Enter
Rewind	Opt+Cmd+R	Alt+Ctrl+R
Test Movie	Cmd+Return	Ctrl+Enter
Debug Movie	Shift+Cmd+Return	Shift+Ctrl+Enter
Test Scene	Opt+Cmd+Return	Alt+Ctrl+Enter
Enable Simple Buttons	Opt+Cmd+B	Alt+Ctrl+B

Window Menu	Mac	PC
New Window	Opt+Cmd+N	Alt+Ctrl+N
Actions	Opt+Cmd+A	Alt+Ctrl+A
Movie Explorer	Opt+Cmd+M	Alt+Ctrl+M
Library	Cmd+L	Ctrl+L

CORIOLIS
Creative Professionals Press

Flash™ 5
Visual Insight

Sherry London

Dan London

Flash™ 5 Visual Insight
© 2001 The Coriolis Group. All rights reserved.

Limits of Liability and Disclaimer of Warranty

Trademarks

The Coriolis Group, LLC
14455 North Hayden Road
Suite 220
Scottsdale, Arizona 85260

(480) 483-0192
FAX: (480) 483-0193
www.coriolis.com

Library of Congress Cataloging-In-Publication Data
London, Sherry.
Flash™ 5 visual insight/ by Sherry London and Dan London.
    p. cm

    ISBN 1-57610-700-0
    1. Computer animation. 2. Flash (Computer file) 3. Web sites--Design. I. London, Dan. II. Title.
TR897.7 .L66 2001
006.6'96--dc21   00-069422
                                CIP

President, CEO
Keith Weiskamp

Publisher
Steve Sayre

Acquisitions Editor
Beth Kohler

Development Editor
Michelle Stroup

Product Marketing Manager
Patricia Davenport

Project Editor
Jennifer Ashley

Technical Reviewer
Jon Shanley

Production Coordinator
Meg E. Turecek

Cover Designer
Jody Winkler

Layout Designer
April Nielsen

Printed in the United States of America
10 9 8 7 6 5 4 3 2 1

A Note from Coriolis

Thank you for choosing this book from The Coriolis Group. Our graphics team strives to meet the needs of creative professionals such as yourself with our three distinctive series: *Visual Insight*, *f/x and Design*, and *In Depth*. We'd love to hear how we're doing in our quest to provide you with information on the latest and most innovative technologies in graphic design, 3D animation, and Web design. Do our books teach you what you want to know? Are the examples illustrative enough? Are there other topics you'd like to see us address?

Please contact us at the address below with your thoughts on this or any of our other books. Should you have any technical questions or concerns about this book, you can contact the Coriolis support team at **techsupport@coriolis.com**; be sure to include this book's title and ISBN, as well as your name, email address, or phone number.

Thank you for your interest in Coriolis books. We look forward to hearing from you.

Coriolis Creative Professionals Press
The Coriolis Group
14455 N. Hayden Road, Suite 220
Scottsdale, AZ 85260

Email: **cpp@coriolis.com**

Phone: (480) 483-0192
Toll free: (800) 410-0192

*Visit our Web site at **creative.coriolis.com** to find the latest information about our current and upcoming graphics books.*

Other Titles for the Creative Professional

Looking Good on the Web
By Daniel Gray

Illustrator® 9 Visual Insight
By T. Michael Clark

Dreamweaver 4 Visual Insight
By Greg Holden, Scott Willis

GoLive™ 5 Visual Insight
By David A. Crowder, Rhonda Crowder

Photoshop® 6 Visual Insight
By Ramona Pruitt, Joshua Pruitt

Paint Shop Pro™ 6 Visual Insight
By Ramona Pruitt, Joshua Pruitt

Illustrator® 9 f/x and Design
By Sherry London

GoLive™ 5 f/x and Design
By Richard Schrand

Painter® 6 f/x and Design
By Sherry London and Rhoda Grossman

Flash™ ActionScript f/x and Design
By Bill Sanders

Flash™ 5 f/x and Design
By Bill Sanders

Flash™ 5 Cartoons and Games f/x and Design
By Bill Turner, James Robertson, and Richard Bazley

Photoshop® 6 In Depth
By David Xenakis, Benjamin Levisay

*To Dan—with love and pride. Raising a son like you is
the most rewarding thing I've done with my life.*
—Sherry London

❧

*To my parents for their constant support
and for never letting me starve.*
—Dan London

❧

About the Authors

Sherry London is an artist and a writer. She has written numerous books on computer graphics, including *Painter 6 f/x and Design* with Rhoda Grossman, and *Illustrator 9 f/x and Design*. She teaches online courses in Photoshop and Flash for Education to Go (**www.ed2go.com**).

Dan London is a singer/songwriter. He currently works for a Web company where he creates Web pages in HTML and Flash. He also maintains a freelance Web design business.

Acknowledgments

No book is ever the product of just one or two people. We owe a debt of thanks to all the many people whose hard work made this book a reality:

- Michelle Stroup, Beth Kohler, Jennifer Ashley, and all the other folks at Coriolis.
- Leona Lapez of Macromedia.
- Scott Hamlin of Eyeland Studios.
- Jennifer Hall and Matthew David, who jumped in when deadlines got too close.

Last, but never least, our agent, Margot Maley-Hutchinson, and all the other wonderful people at Waterside Productions.

—*Sherry London and Dan London*

Contents at a Glance

Table of Contents

Introduction

About Macromedia Flash 5

Flash was originally released as *FutureSplash* and was the first program to animate vector output for the Web. Macromedia purchased the program and has been making waves with it since.

Flash has taken the Web by storm. It provides a cross-platform, browser-independent way to generate interactive animations that have a small file size. Unlike dynamic HTML, Flash plays anywhere that the Flash plugin is installed. The Flash plugin is readily available and used in over 80 percent of Web browsers installed on user machines.

In Flash 4, Macromedia introduced a scripting language with conditional **if** statements to enable programmers to create more interactive Flash sites. In Flash 5, Macromedia has enhanced the language (called ActionScript) and given it new Java-like syntax, making it much more accessible and powerful for experienced programmers. For graphic artists, Flash 5 introduces the Bézier Pen, which makes shapes much easier to edit.

Who Needs This Book

If you're just getting started with Flash site design, this book will take you from the most basic necessities as far as you can go without having to become a programmer. The book is aimed at graphics folks, and shows how to create animated content for sites. Although you'll learn a little bit about using simple Actions, no programming skills are required.

If you do need to (or want to) learn Flash programming, Coriolis also publishes *Flash ActionScript f/x and Design*, which provides a more in-depth look at ActionScript.

Visual Insight Philosophy

The Visual Insight series of books from Coriolis is geared to presenting practical knowledge in a visually appealing format that makes learning easy. Each process in the book is clearly described step by step, and each step is carefully illustrated to show exactly how to accomplish the tasks involved.

The Visual Insight books are presented in a two-column format, with steps listed on the left side of the page and the accompanying figures on the right side, next to the steps they illustrate. The steps get right to the point, making sure that you waste no time in getting done what you need to get done.

This Book's Structure

This book is composed of two parts. Part I, Techniques and Tasks, is composed of Chapters 1 through 9. This part deals with the nitty-gritty details of working with Flash. Part I presents, in down-to-earth language, the precise methods and procedures you need to follow to make Flash do what you want. Each chapter's topic is progressively more advanced, beginning with a chapter on understanding the Flash user interface and leading up to a chapter on publishing and optimizing Web sites with Flash.

Part II, Projects, is composed of Chapters 10 through 15. This part contains a series of projects that expand on the knowledge gained in Part I. Each project deals with how to use Flash to solve common real-life Web-design situations, such as creating custom Web pages, working with layers, creating buttons, and making drop-down menus.

Flash "newbies" are probably best off starting with Chapter 1 and working their way through the book chapter by chapter. Other users might want to dive into the table of contents or index and go right to the areas that they need to use right away.

In either case, this book is designed to give you a good grounding in Flash 5. Turn the page, and begin creating.

Part I

Techniques and Tasks

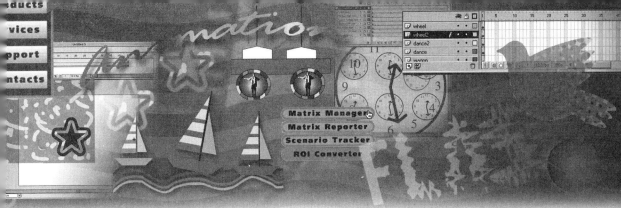

Chapter 1
Basic Tools

- Learn to navigate the Flash interface

- Open, create, and save images

- Become familiar with the basic tools and functions

- Learn to set program preferences

By Sherry London

A First Look at Flash

Macromedia Flash 5 is a very complex program that enables you to create sophisticated Web animations and applications that are cross-platform and cross-browser and that download quickly and reliably. Although Flash 5 contains an advanced-level scripting language, you can create many sites without needing to program at all. As you'll see, Flash has many tools that an artist can use quite easily.

The best place to start learning Flash is to look at its interface and see how the various tools work. In this chapter, you'll learn about the Flash interface and meet the various tools, palettes, and preference settings. You'll take a very brief look at some of the animation items, but you'll learn much more about those later in the book.

Opening Flash

The first time you open Flash, you'll see a tutorial entitled *Welcome to Flash 5*. Flash ships with excellent tutorials that are worth working through. Each tutorial is in its own Flash movie. Choosing File|Close (Cmd/Ctrl+W) or clicking the Close box closes only the current movie (each Flash document is considered a *movie*).

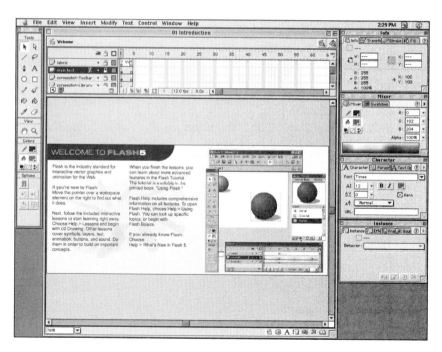

You can view the tutorials at any time by choosing Help|Lessons.

Exploring the Interface

After closing the tutorial, you're ready to create or open a Flash movie. The main components of the Flash work environment are various toolbars, palettes, and menu items that enable you to create exciting projects. Note the following components:

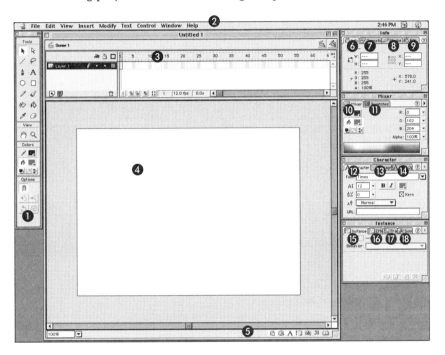

1. Toolbar
2. Menu bar
3. Timeline
4. Stage
5. Launcher bar
6. Info palette
7. Transform palette
8. Stroke palette
9. Fill palette
10. Mixer palette
11. Swatches palette
12. Character palette
13. Paragraph palette
14. Text Options palette
15. Instance palette
16. Effects palette
17. Frame palette
18. Sound palette

Tooltips

Holding the mouse cursor over any icon for a few seconds brings up a tooltip message, which tells you the name of the icon and the Shortcut key, if there is one. Tooltips are helpful because Flash has so many icons that you can all too easily forget what each one does.

The Stage

The stage is where you create your movie and where the action happens. Macromedia Flash owes much of its original inspiration to Macromedia Director, and the stage metaphor is one of its borrowed concepts. The stage appears directly under the Timeline. All your image elements live on the stage, and the size of the stage determines the size of your movie.

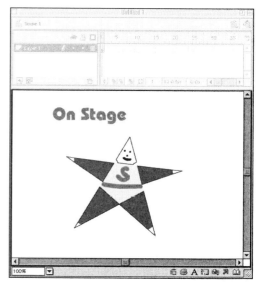

The Tool Interface

The Toolbox is "control central" for creating images. All the painting and drawing tools are in the Toolbox. The Toolbox itself is divided into four sections: Tools, View, Colors, and Options. The Options change based on the active tool. Icons help you remember the tool's function:

Tools

1. Selection (Arrow) tool

2. Line tool

3. Pen tool

4. Oval tool

5. Pencil tool

6. Ink Bottle tool

7. Eyedropper tool

8. Subselect tool

9. Lasso tool

10. Text tool

11. Rectangle tool

12. Paintbrush tool

13. Paintbucket tool

14. Eraser tool

View

1. Hand tool

2. Zoom tool

Colors

1. Stroke Color selector

2. Fill Color selector

3. Default Colors, No Stroke or Fill, and Swap Fill and Stroke

Options

1. Snap

2. Smooth

3. Straighten

4. Rotate

5. Scale

About Movies

Flash calls its files *movies*, so when you open a file for editing, you are opening a *movie*. Flash lets you open, create, edit, save, and change properties of movies.

Opening Movies

To open an existing file, choose File|Open. A dialog box shows the files on your hard drive. Flash will open a variety of file types. Flash movies that have not been compiled have an .fla extension and movies that are ready to be placed on the Web have a .swf extension.

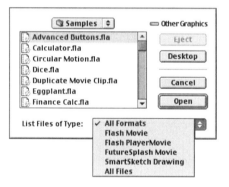

Creating a New Movie

To create a new movie, choose File|New. A new movie document opens using the defaults set at the Movie Property dialog box.

Setting Movie Properties

To change the properties of a movie, choose Modify|Movie (Cmd/Ctrl+M). In the Movie Properties dialog box, you'll find these options:

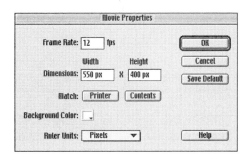

- *Frame Rate*—Determines how fast the movie plays. The optimal speed for Web viewing is 12 frames per second (fps), which is the default.

- *Dimensions*—Changes the movie height and/or width.

- *Match*—Sets the movie size to match either the contents of the stage or the size of your printer paper (minus the margin setting). You can make a tiny movie by placing all your objects near the top-left corner of the stage. If you design a form, you might want to match the size of the paper on which it should be printed.

- *Background Color*—Changes the color of the background. Click the Background Color swatch and select a new color from the sample colors that appear.

- *Ruler Units*—Determines ruler units. This setting also affects the units in the Info palette.

- *Save Default*—Saves your new settings as the defaults.

Saving Movies

Choose File|Save or File|Save As to save your movie. The only format available is Flash Movie. If you're working on a Mac, you might want to add the .fla suffix so you can exchange files with the Windows version.

Exporting Movies

You can export animations in a variety of formats with the Export Movie command. In addition to the Flash Player format, your choices range from a PICT sequence to a QuickTime movie. The file types you can export are somewhat different on the Mac than they are in Windows.

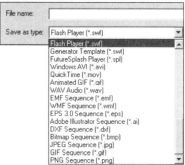

Exporting Images

To save the current view of the movie as a static image, choose File|Export Image. From the Format drop-down box, select your desired format. You can save in all the standard Web formats, including GIF, JPEG, and PNG. You can also save files in Adobe Illustrator, DXF, EPS, and a variety of raster formats. The Windows version also lets you export in Windows Metafile and Enhanced Metafile formats.

Publish and Publish Settings

Flash lets you generate output for multiple formats at one time by using the Publish command. Before selecting File|Publish, complete the dialog boxes in File|Publish Settings. The dialog box is divided into three separate tabbed panels: Formats, Flash, and HTML.

The Publish Settings|Formats Tab

The Flash and HTML options are checked by default in the Formats panel, but you can change the combination of files to generate. You can rename the files, select from a variety of formats, or decide whether you want Flash to generate the HTML for you automatically.

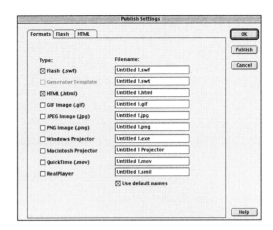

The Publish Settings|Flash Tab

At the Flash tab, you set export options for publishing Flash movies. You'll learn more about these options in Chapter 9. You can control many export features, such as enabling remote users to debug the generated version of the movie (.swf file) or enabling viewers to import your generated movie into Flash to modify or duplicate your work. You can also set the JPEG quality for images that export as raster objects and adjust your sound settings.

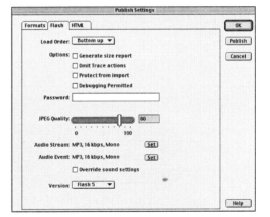

The Publish Settings|HTML Tab

When you add Flash movies to a Web page, you need to create the HTML that makes the page visible on the Web. You set HTML options in the HTML dialog box of the Publish Settings command. You'll learn more about this dialog box in Chapter 9. The HTML panel gathers all your options so that Flash can generate an HTML page and an Embed tag to display the movie. You change the HTML code by changing the template you select in the Template field.

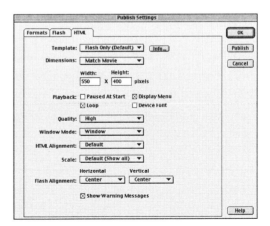

Choosing Colors

Flash provides many different ways to select color. Color dialog boxes appear in many different palettes and commands. In most cases, the actual color picker is identical. You can also select specific colors to be used as the Stroke or the Fill of an object from three places: the Stroke or Fill selectors on the Toolbox, the drop-down color selectors on the Stroke or Fill palettes, or the Stroke and Fill colors in the Mixer. The Mixer and the Stroke and Fill palettes give you additional options.

Color Palettes

In every color dialog box, Flash provides the same palette to select colors from. You'll see this palette used for Stroke and Fill, the Mixer, the Stroke and Fill palettes, and the Effects palettes. Features of the palette are listed below.

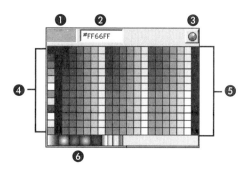

1. Color swatch

2. Hexadecimal color number

3. Launch System color picker

4. Primary and secondary colors; Six Step Black-to-White

5. Web-safe colors

6. Available gradients

Selecting a Color

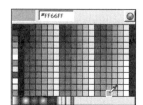

To pick a color from the palette, drag your cursor over the palette. The cursor changes into an Eyedropper. You can pick up color from anywhere in the palette or in the application. Although the Hexadecimal color field registers color from anywhere on your monitor, you can't pick up colors from outside Flash—clicking the desired "outside" color transfers you out of Flash.

Web-Safe Colors

Web-safe colors display as solid colors on browsers both on the Mac and in Windows and on monitors that display only 256 colors. Mac and Windows share a common palette of 216 colors. The characteristic of a Web-safe color is that the hexadecimal numbers are all "triplets"—six letters or digits in repeating groups of two. Further, the digits are all multiples of 3 and the letters are either C or F. For example, without knowing anything about color #FF3366, you know it's Web-safe, whereas #11BB55 or #6283AD2 are not.

Swatches Palette

The Swatches palette enables you to keep a version of the drop-down Color palette open and clickable at all times. You can resize the palette and drag the separator bar to change the spacing between the swatch area and the gradient area. You can also add, delete, and edit colors; save the colors; change the default color set; and store and manage custom color sets. You can create non-Web-safe colors in the Mixer and then store the swatch in the Swatches palette.

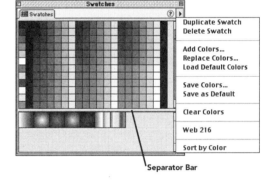

Separator Bar

Colors: Stroke and Fill on the Toolbox

Before you choose a drawing or shape tool, set your stroke and fill colors in the Toolbox. Click the small arrowhead near the bottom-right of either the Stroke or the Fill control to open the Color palette. The colors in the Toolbox are used when you create a new object. To change the color of the Stroke or the Fill of an object, you can use the same area of the Toolbox, but you need to select the object first.

Setting Colors to the Default

You can change your Stroke and Fill colors back to black and white by clicking the Default Color icon on the Toolbox.

Setting Colors to None

To create objects that lack either a Stroke or a Fill color, select the None option *before* you create your object. The None icon works with whichever color selector is active in the Toolbox and removes all color from the active color control. However, after creating an object, your only method of removing a stroke or fill is to select and delete it. Also, the None option is available only when the Oval tool or the Rectangle tool is selected. The Color palette has no None option.

Swapping Stroke and Fill Colors

Click the double-pointed arrow icon in the Toolbox to exchange your stroke and fill colors.

The Stroke Panel

You can select the size, color, and style of your strokes in the Stroke panel. If the Stroke panel isn't visible, choose Window|Panels|Stroke Panel.

Using the Stroke Panel

On the Stroke panel, you can enter the Stroke width and open the Stroke Color palette.

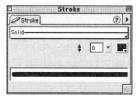

Choosing a Line Style

You can select a line style from a list of preset styles. Any stroke that is not solid, however, may make your file unacceptably large.

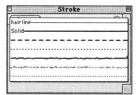

The Custom Line Style Option

Click the arrowhead at the right of the Stroke panel to build a custom style. A custom style enables you to specify many different parameters for a stroke.

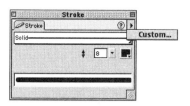

Building a Custom Line Style

First, select the specific type of effect you want from the Type drop-down menu: Solid, Dashed, Dotted, Ragged, Stipple, or Hatched. Once you've selected the basic style other options that are specific for each base style appear. They let you determine exactly how you want your new custom stroke to look. When you click OK, your stroke is added to the Stroke drop-down list.

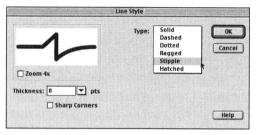

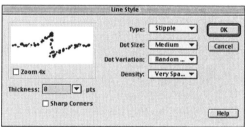

The Fill Panel

The Fill panel enables you to select the type and color of a Fill. It also gives you access to the Gradient Editor. If the Fill panel isn't visible, choose Window|Panels|Fill Panel.

Choosing a Fill Type and Color

In the Fill panel, you can open the same Color selection palette that is in the Toolbox. If no object is selected, you'll set the Fill for the next object you create. If an object is selected, you'll change its fill color. Your Fill type options are None, Solid, Linear Gradient, Radial Gradient, and Bitmap. You'll learn about bitmap fills in Chapter 2.

Creating a Gradient

When you select a Linear or Radial Gradient in the Fill panel, the Gradient Editor appears. Features of the Gradient Editor are listed below.

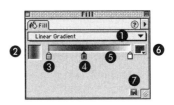

1. Select a Linear or Radial Gradient.

2. See a preview swatch of the gradient you are creating.

3. Change the sliders, which hold the colors for the gradient. Click under the Gradient Bar (5) to create a new slider. The triangle on top of the new slider is white, which means it is not selected. You can change the color only of a selected slider.

4. Select a slider, by clicking it. Its top will turn black.

5. Move the sliders anywhere along the Gradient Bar by dragging them.

6. Click the Color Selector to choose a new color for a selected slider.

7. Click the icon to save the gradient with your current movie and add it to the Swatches palette. However, it won't appear when you open a new movie.

The Mixer Palette

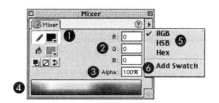

The Mixer palette combines the Stroke and Fill color selection palettes, a visual color ramp, and a numeric color selector.

1. *Stroke and Fill area*—The same area as in the Toolbox.

2. *Numeric Color mixer*—Allows you to enter specific color numbers.

3. *Alpha selector*—Controls the opacity of the Fill or Stroke; an Alpha of 100 percent is opaque.

4. *Visual Color bar*—Contains all the colors in a specific color space.

5. *Color Space selector*—Lets you define colors as RGB, HSB, or Hex.

6. *Add Swatch option*—Adds the selected color to the Swatches palette.

Drawing Tools

Flash provides Pencil, Paintbrush, and Eraser tools for drawing (and editing) freeform objects. Each tool has a different set of options. You set colors for the tools by using the various color selection palettes that are discussed above.

Pencil Tool

The Pencil tool draws freeform lines with the Stroke color you select in the Toolbox or the Stroke color palette. To use the Pencil tool, select the Stroke color, set the Stroke attributes in the Stroke panel, and choose your Pencil Options in the Toolbox. To draw a line, move your cursor over the stage while keeping the mouse button pressed.

Selecting a Pencil Tool Stroke Size

You can change the Pencil tool size only by changing the Stroke width in the Stroke panel. Click the arrowhead next to the numeric stroke width field to access a slider that controls the stroke width.

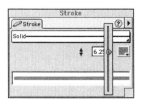

Selecting Pencil Tool Options

The Pencil tool lets you compensate for the jitter you might leave in an object when you draw freehand with a Pencil.

1. *Ink*—Leaves your drawing untouched.

2. *Smooth*—Turns jagged lines into curves.

3. *Straighten*—Makes lines straighter; it also recognizes geometric objects such as rectangles, ovals, and triangles. With this option turned on, any shape that looks vaguely rounded becomes an accurate oval.

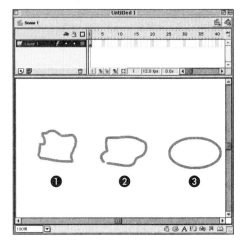

Paintbrush Tool

The Paintbrush tool uses the Fill color set in the Toolbox. It lets you paint, freehand, filled objects of various sizes using various methods of applying paint. To use the tool, drag it as you would a "real" brush over the stage while pressing the mouse button. Although your shape might look ragged as you draw it, Flash smoothes out the shape when you finish.

1. Paint Mode

2. Brush Size

3. Brush Shape

4. Lock Fill

Setting the Paintbrush Tool Size

The second selection on the Options palette drops down to reveal eight brush sizes. Drag your cursor to highlight the brush size you want.

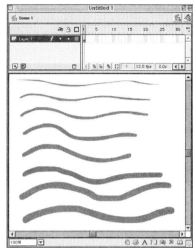

Setting the Paintbrush Tool Shape

Select a different shape for the brush tool by opening the Brush Shape options menu. Each brush shape adds a unique look to your hand-drawn object.

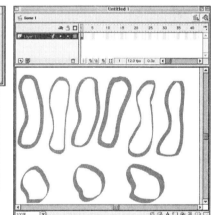

Selecting Paintbrush Tool Paint Modes

Flash has several unique ways for the Paintbrush tool to interact with the objects already on the stage.

1. *Paint Normal*—Paint covers everything it's brushed over.

2. *Paint Fills*—Paint covers only fills or areas without objects. You can see the flower's stroke through the new paint.

3. *Paint Behind*—Paint covers only areas that are not part of an object.

4. *Paint Selection*—Paint covers only the area that you brush, if that area is part of a selection.

5. *Paint Inside*—Paint covers only the fill of the object. It is an excellent method for "coloring within the lines."

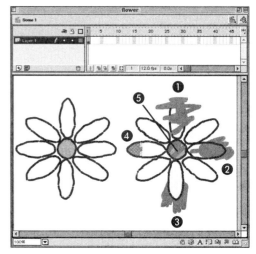

Locking a Fill

Locking a gradient or bitmapped fill to the stage lets you create many different objects that look as if they are all part of the same fill. If you create an object with a gradient fill first and then lock the fill, subsequent objects lock to the object that you first filled.

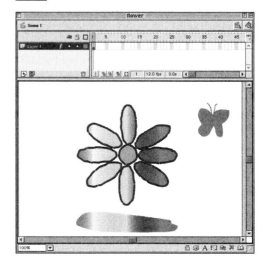

Eraser Tool

The Eraser tool lets you remove portions of objects. You can erase everything on the stage by double-clicking the Eraser tool.

Selecting the Eraser Tool Shape

You can change the shape and size of the Eraser tool to any one of 10 combinations of square or round erasers in five sizes. Select your desired eraser from the drop-down Shape and Size selector in the Options section of the Toolbox. You need to select the Eraser tool before Options becomes visible.

Selecting Eraser Tool Modes

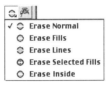

Eraser tool features are similar to Paintbrush features.

1. *Erase Normal*—The Eraser erases anything.

2. *Erase Fills*—The Eraser works only on filled areas of objects.

3. *Erase Lines*—The Eraser erases only strokes.

4. *Erase Selected Fills*—First, select all or part of an object. The Eraser tool removes the area within the selection over which you drag your cursor. This mode removes only fill, not strokes.

5. *Erase Inside*—The Eraser removes fill only from the object where your brush stroke begins.

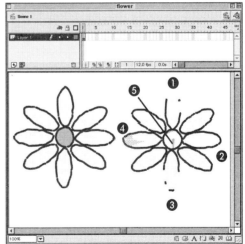

Turning On the Faucet

The Faucet option turns the Eraser into a tool with one-click convenience. You can erase an entire fill or stroke segment with one click—depending on where you click with the Eraser.

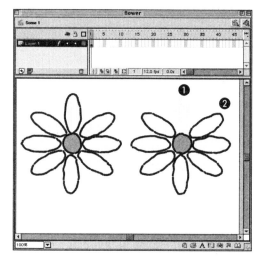

1. If you click a stroke, you'll erase the entire segment.

2. If you click a fill, the entire fill disappears.

The Shape Tools

Flash enables you to draw many different types of shapes. You can create and combine geometric primitives, such as the ellipse, circle, square, and rectangle, to build more complex forms. You can also use the new Pen tool, which creates shapes that use Bézier curves like those created in FreeHand or Illustrator.

To create an unfilled or unstroked shape, select None as the stroke or fill color before you draw the shape. Otherwise, you must select and delete the unwanted stroke or fill after the shape is drawn. Selecting None as a fill or stroke after a shape is created doesn't change the stroke or fill of the shape.

Pen Tool

The Pen tool creates straight or curved lines between anchor points. An anchor point appears every time you click the mouse. To create a new shape, click where you want the next anchor point to appear and adjust the angle of the curve before you set the next anchor point. You create a closed shape by ending the path at your origin point.

Anatomy of a Bézier Curve

A Bézier curve is a complex system of shape control. It consists of paths (line or curve segments) that are shaped by anchor points and tangent handles. Bézier curve features include:

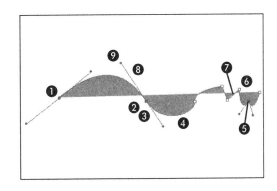

1. *Origin Point*—Begins the path.

2. *Anchor Point*—Appears when you click the mouse.

3. *Smooth Point*—Is created by dragging the mouse as you set an anchor point.

4. *Curve Segment*—Appears between two smooth anchor points.

5. *Cusp*—Appears if you reshape tangent lines (8) independently.

6. *Corner Point*—Appears if you click to set an anchor point without dragging.

7. *Line Segment*—Appears between two corner points.

8. *Tangent Line*—Controls the direction of the curve segments.

9. *Tangent Handle*—Lets you adjust the tangent lines.

Drawing Curved Segments

With the Pen tool, click where you want the first curve to start. Holding down the button, drag the mouse in the direction you want the next curve to lie, then release the mouse button. The curve's tangent handles appear. Shift-drag to constrain the tangent handles to move in multiples of 45 degrees. Move the tangent handle to adjust the curve after the shape is drawn. Set your next point by clicking and dragging in the direction you want the curve to move.

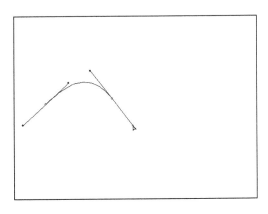

Drawing Line Segments

With the Pen tool, click where you want the first line to start. Don't hold down the button as you drag. Set your next point by clicking where you want the line to end. Shift-drag to constrain the line's anchor points to movements in multiples of 45 degrees.

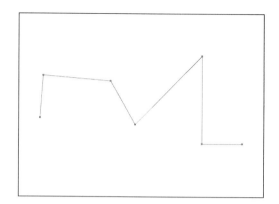

Oval Tool

The Oval tool draws ovals and circles.

Drawing an Oval

Choose the Oval tool. Click anywhere on the stage and drag the Oval tool until the figure is the desired size.

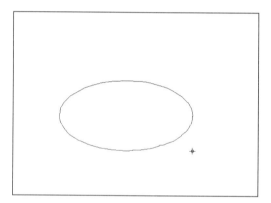

Drawing a Circle

To draw a circle, use the Oval tool. Either hold the Shift key as you drag or watch the cursor shape and release the mouse button when the cursor changes to a circle attached to an outside quadrant of a cross (an oval has the cross cursor through the circle).

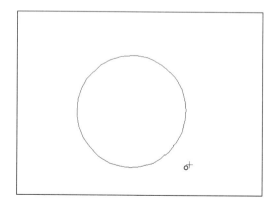

Rectangle Tool

The Rectangle tool draws rectangles, squares, and round-cornered rectangles.

Drawing a Rectangle

Choose the Rectangle tool. Click anywhere on the stage and drag the Rectangle tool until the figure is the desired size.

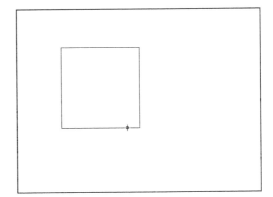

Drawing a Square

To draw a square, use the Rectangle tool. Either hold the Shift key as you drag or watch the cursor shape and release the mouse button when the cursor changes to a circle attached to an outside quadrant of a cross (a rectangle has the cross cursor through the circle).

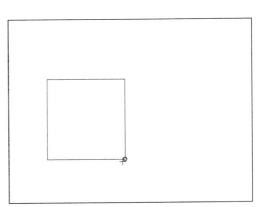

Drawing a Round-Cornered Rectangle

To draw a round-cornered rectangle, click the Radius option at the bottom of the Toolbox and set the Corner Radius in the dialog box that appears. Then use the Rectangle tool and drag your round-cornered rectangle. Press the arrow keys as you draw to increase (down arrow) or decrease (up arrow) the Corner Radius size.

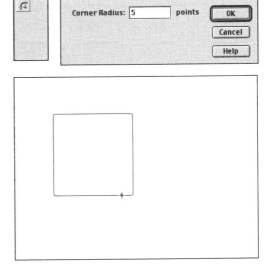

Line Tool

You can draw single lines with the Line tool. Click where you want each line to start and drag the line until it is the length and direction you want. Hold the Shift key as you click to constrain the line movements to multiples of 45 degrees or watch the cursor shape and release the mouse button when the cursor changes to a circle attached to an outside quadrant of a cross. You cannot fill a line.

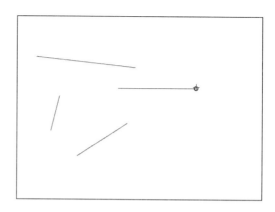

The Fill Tools

The Fill tools consist of the Paint Bucket and the Ink Bottle.

Ink Bottle Tool

Use the Ink Bottle tool to change the stroke of an object. First select the stroke color, width, and style from the Stroke Colors icon on the Toolbox or the Stroke panel. Then place your cursor against the edge of the shape and click. If the object has a stroke, it will be changed; if it doesn't, one will be added. (You don't need to select the object first.)

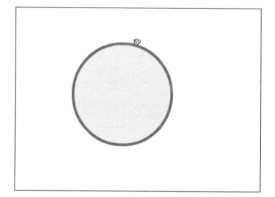

Paint Bucket Tool

Use the Paint Bucket tool to change the fill of an object. First select the fill color and style from the Fill Colors icon on the Toolbox or the Fill panel. Then place your cursor against the edge of the shape and click. If the object has a fill, it will be changed; if it doesn't, one will be added. (You don't need to select the object first.)

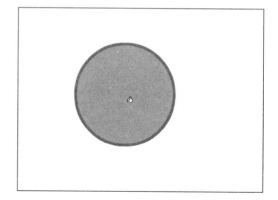

Angling a Gradient Fill

If you use the Paint Bucket tool to fill an object with a gradient, you can change the gradient angle as you fill the shape. Instead of clicking with the Paint Bucket tool, click and hold down the mouse button to drag the Paint Bucket the distance and angle of your desired gradient. When the cursor line is in position, release the mouse button.

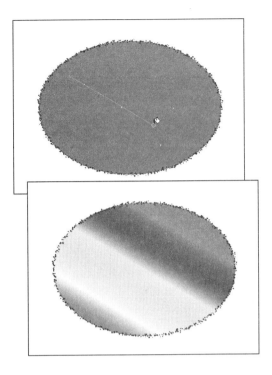

Gap Size Option

The Paint Bucket tool can fill stroked areas even if the stroke contains gaps. Unlike most graphics programs, you can instruct Flash to "not see" gaps of various sizes so that fill doesn't leak through the gaps. Click the Fill Gap option to open a menu where you can select the size of the gap Flash sees as solid. Then fill the object with the Paint Bucket tool.

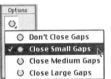

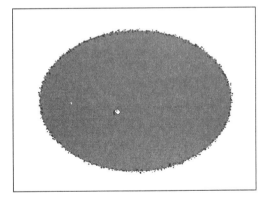

Scaling a Gradient Fill with the Transform Fill Option

You can use the Transform Fill option on the Paint Bucket tool to change the midpoint of a gradient fill. Choose the Paint Bucket tool and click the Transform Fill icon on the Toolbox. Select an object. To change the scale of the gradient, drag the center handle on the lines that appear.

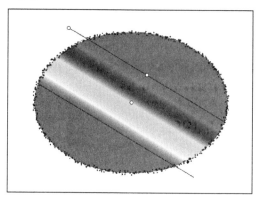

Rotating a Gradient Fill with the Transform Fill Option

You can use the Transform Fill option on the Paint Bucket tool to change the angle of a gradient fill. Choose the Paint Bucket tool and click the Transform Fill icon on the Toolbox. Select an object. Place your cursor over the large circle at the end of the line and rotate the gradient to the desired angle. The cursor displays a larger O when the angle is a multiple of 45 degrees.

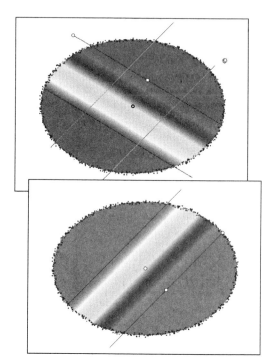

Altering a Bitmap Fill with the Transform Fill Option

You can use the Transform Fill option on the Paint Bucket tool to change a number of characteristics of a bitmap fill, as explained below.

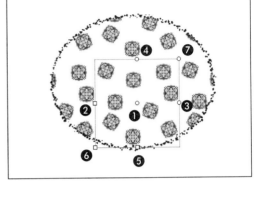

1. Moves the location of the bitmap fill.

2. Stretches the bitmap fill horizontally.

3. Skews the bitmap fill vertically.

4. Skews the bitmap fill horizontally.

5. Stretches the bitmap fill vertically.

6. Enlarges or compresses the bitmap fill proportionally.

7. Rotates the bitmap fill.

The Selection Tools

The Selection tools are the Arrow tool, the Subselect tool (hollow arrow), and the Lasso tool. You will learn more about these tools in Chapter 2.

The View Tools

The Hand tool and the Zoom tool constitute the View tools group in the Toolbox. They let you move the view of your image within the drawing space and enlarge the view of the image. Neither tool changes the actual drawing in any way.

The Hand Tool

The Hand tool lets you change the position of the image on the stage in your viewing area. It works when the window through which you view the stage is smaller than the actual stage. To use the Hand tool, either select it from the Toolbox or press the spacebar with a different tool selected. Then click an image and drag.

The Zoom Tool

The Zoom tool lets you change the visible size of your image on your monitor. Zooming in shows you less of the stage but more detail. Zooming out shows you more of the stage but less detail. Zooming changes only the view, not the image itself. The Zoom tool has two modifiers—one to zoom in (+) and one to zoom out (-). Use the Zoom tool without selecting it by pressing Opt/Alt+spacebar to zoom in or Opt+Cmd/Alt+Ctrl+spacebar to zoom out.

Customizing Your Work Environment

You can customize your work environment by rearranging the windows and panels on your monitor, selecting a variety of Preferences, and choosing the set of keyboard commands to use.

Setting Preferences

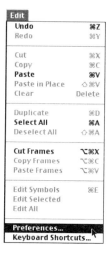

To change the Preferences for Flash, choose Edit|Preferences. You can change the General, Editing, and Clipboard preferences.

General Preferences

The General preferences tab allows you to set a number of options:

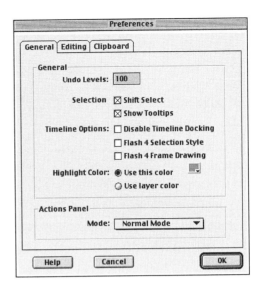

- Set the Undo Level to a number between 0 and 200. The more Undo Levels you permit, the more RAM you need.

- Choose the Shift Select checkbox if you want to press the Shift key to add multiple objects to a selection. This option gives you additional control; If the box is not checked, every time you click an object you add it to a selection. Choosing Shift Select lets you click an object *without* adding it to a selection; the Shift key must be pressed to add to the selection.

- Select the Show Tooltips checkbox to see tooltips when the cursor moves over an icon.

- Select the Disable Timeline Docking checkbox to keep the Timeline from hugging the application window if you separate the Timeline from the stage.

- Select Flash 4 Selection Style or Flash 4 Frame Drawing to emulate the behavior of those elements from Flash 4. When this option isn't checked, black keyframes don't show hollow circles.

- Click Use This Color to select a Highlight Color from the adjacent box. Clicking Use Layer Color uses the current layer's outline color as the layer highlight.

- Select Normal Mode in the Actions Panel option to create Actions using prompts. Select Expert Mode to create actions by entering ActionScript commands in the Actions panel.

Editing Preferences

The Editing preferences tab lets you set a number of options that change the way you use the Pen and the Drawing tools:

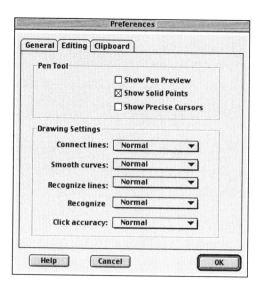

- *Show Pen Preview*—Previews path segments before you set the end of the path.

- *Show Solid Points*—Makes the unselected anchor points appear solid and the selected one appear hollow; unselecting this option reverses this pattern.

- *Show Precise Cursors*—Changes the Pen Tool icon into a crosshair as you draw the path.

- *Connect Lines*—Sets a tolerance for connecting lines when you draw. The setting determines whether lines snap to nearby lines.

- *Smooth Curves*—Lets you select the behavior of the Pencil tool with the Smooth or Straighten option on.

- *Recognize Lines*—Sets the level of recognition for horizontal or vertical lines and determines how close to straight they must be before Flash makes them perfectly straight.

- *Recognize*—Determines how accurately you must draw a geometric shape before Flash recognizes it and replaces it with an accurate shape.

- *Click Accuracy*—Determines how close your cursor must be to an object before Flash realizes you want to click it.

Clipboard Preferences

The options at the Clipboard preferences tab affect the way Flash treats objects on the Clipboard. On Windows, you specify the resolution and bit-depth of bitmaps pasted to the clipboard and the quality of gradient fills placed in a Windows metafile. On the Mac, you specify whether PICT images on the clipboard are to be treated as vector or raster data and whether to include Postscript. For both platforms, you specify whether text pasted from FreeHand is editable.

Selecting Keyboard Command Shortcuts

Flash 5 lets you change the keyboard shortcuts for Drawing menu commands, Drawing tools, and Test Movie commands. You can use shortcuts based on sets in Fireworks, FreeHand, Illustrator, or Photoshop as well as Flash 5 commands. You can also create your own sets and alter any command by choosing it in the appropriate list.

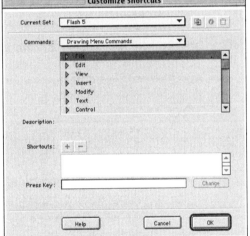

Arranging Panels

Flash keeps a default set of arrangements for
the panels that are part of the program (Stroke,
Fill, Color, etc.). You can change the arrangements by dragging a panel out of its container.
If you like the arrangement, you can save it
as a new panel set by choosing Save Panel
Layout from the Window menu.

Getting Help

Flash 5 has an extensive help system. The Help files include the Flash manual as well as ActionScript
syntax and reference help. You can access Help by choosing Help|Using Flash. You can then read
through the manual, access the index of the manual, or search for a specific reference.

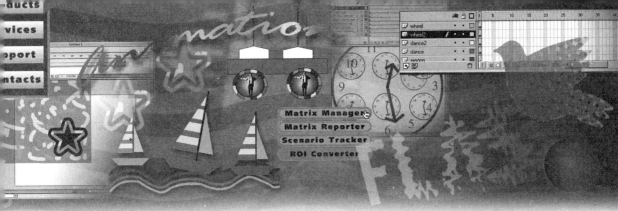

Chapter 2
Drawing in Flash

- Learn to create, select, and move objects

- Change an object's scale or orientation

- Create and manipulate object groups

- Import vector and bitmapped images

- Break apart text

By Sherry London

Selecting Objects

Flash graphics are made to be moved. To move an object, you need to select it first. Flash allows you to select objects in a number of different ways. In Chapter 1, you learned how to create objects. Now, you'll learn how to select them so that you can change and manipulate them.

The Arrow Tool

The Arrow tool enables you to select an entire object, stroke, or fill.

Selecting Object Fills

You can create this filled star with the Paint-brush tool. It has no stroke. Use the Arrow tool to select it by clicking the object. On a simple shape such as this, the Arrow tool selects the entire star. You can tell it's selected because it's filled with small dots.

Selecting Strokes

If you create an outline around the star by fill-ing the edge of the shape with the Ink Bottle, clicking once to select the stroke selects only a portion of it. You can select the entire stroke by double-clicking it. Flash lets you select an object's stroke and fill separately.

Selection Rectangle

You can drag a selection rectangle with the Arrow tool to enclose multiple objects or portions of objects.

Selecting Multiple Objects

Flash has no "actual" selection rectangle tool. However, if you have one or more objects on the stage and use the Arrow tool, you can drag an imaginary marquee around the objects to select them. The selection rectangle marquee selects all objects it encloses.

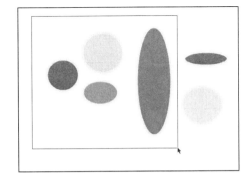

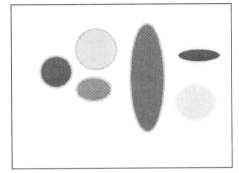

Selecting Portions of Objects

In Flash, you can select parts of an object. If you drag the imaginary marquee around part of some of the objects, only the portions of the objects inside the selection rectangle become selected. If you have worked with Illustrator or FreeHand, you'll find this behavior very different than the normal vector way of working.

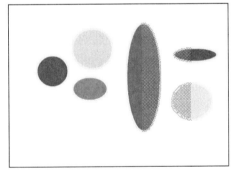

The Lasso Tool

You can also select portions of objects with the Lasso tool. To use the Lasso tool, drag the tool in the shape you want. If you encircle an entire object, you'll select the whole thing. If you enclose a portion of an object, or if you meander through portions of several objects, you select only the pieces you enclose.

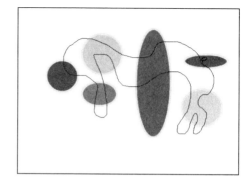

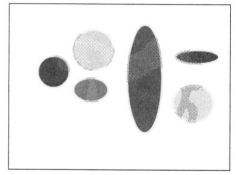

The Subselect Tool

With the new Subselect tool, you can reveal the Bézier points on an object even if you didn't use the Pen tool to create the object. When you click an object with the Subselect tool, you'll see small hollow points on the object. Hollow points indicate that the object is selected but the points are not yet editable. Unlike other selection methods, the selected object doesn't fill with dots.

If you have trouble selecting an object with the Subselect tool, click near the outer edge of the object.

Adding to Selections

You can make discontinuous selections with any of the selection methods. To add to a selection, just press and hold the Shift key as you make a new selection. You can add to a selection using any tool except the Subselect tool. You can use a tool that's different than the tools used to make the previous selections.

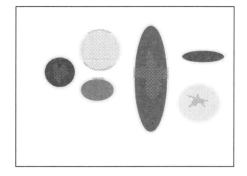

Manipulating Shapes

Flash has several ways to scale, skew, and rotate objects. You can use the Options that become active in the toolbar after you select a shape (if you keep the selection tool active). You can also manipulate shapes by using the Transform palette or the Transform command on the Modify menu.

Setting an Object's Scale

You can scale an object to make it larger or smaller.

1.

The easiest way to scale an object is to choose the Arrow tool and select an object. You can then select Scale from the Options portion of the Toolbox. As soon as you select the Scale option, you'll see eight large hollow boxes called *handles*. This option is equivalent to the bounding box in Illustrator or FreeHand.

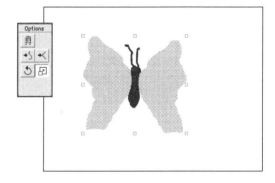

2.

Place your cursor over one of the handles. Press and hold the mouse button and drag the handle in the direction you want to resize the image. Resize the object proportionally by dragging a corner handle. Dragging away from the object enlarges it and dragging toward the object makes the object smaller.

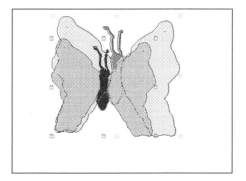

3.

Place your cursor over a center handle on the top, bottom, or sides of the object to scale it disproportionally. You can make the object wider or narrower by dragging a side handle. You can make the object shorter or taller by dragging a top or bottom handle. The object resizes from the handle opposite to the one you drag.

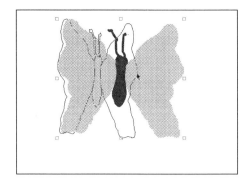

4.

You can choose Modify|Transform|Scale to display the same eight handle boxes. Flash places a checkmark next to the Scale command on the menu when the option is active. You can turn it off by choosing Modify|Transform|Scale again.

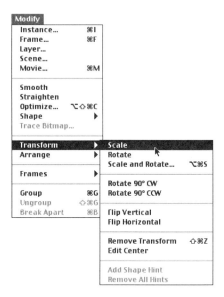

Scaling with the Transform Palette

You can also scale your object using the Transform palette. The top line on the palette controls the width and height by percentages. The first box on the left is the width; the one to the right of it is for the height. If you check the Constrain checkbox, you can enlarge or reduce the object proportionally. You need only enter one percentage; the other box changes to that number as well.

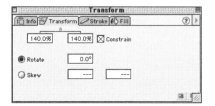

Setting Orientation

You can also change the orientation of your object by rotating, skewing, or flipping it.

1.

The easiest way to rotate an object is to choose the Arrow tool, select the object, and select the Rotate icon from the Options portion of the Toolbox. When you select the Rotate option, you'll see eight large hollow circles. Rotate the object freely by dragging any corner circle. If you press and hold the Shift key as you rotate the object, you can constrain it to rotate in 45-degree increments.

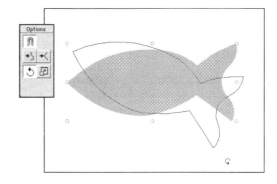

2.

If you move a center handle on the top, bottom, or sides of the object with the Rotate option active, you'll *skew* the object. Skewing an object distorts it as if you were forcing the shape to conform to the inside of a parallelogram.

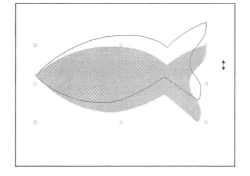

3.

You can flip objects horizontally and vertically by choosing Modify|Transform and then either Flip Vertical or Flip Horizontal from the drop-down menu. You can also activate the Rotate command from the Modify|Transform menu in the same way as the Scale option. In addition, you can turn on both the Scale and the Rotate options at the same time and constrain the object rotation to 90 degrees clockwise or counterclockwise.

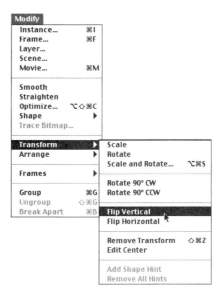

Modifying Transformations

You can edit the center point of your object or remove transformations entirely.

1.

You can change the point from which the object rotates. With the object selected, choose Modify|Transform|Edit Center. A cross marking the center of the object will appear on the object itself. Move it to where you want the new center point to be.

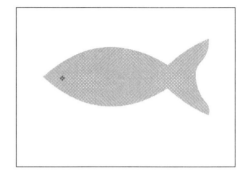

2.

After you've edited the center of your object, the handles for the Scale or Rotate options are small and black instead of hollow, larger, and blue. The object now rotates from the new location that you specified as the "center."

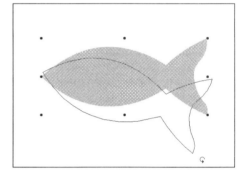

3.

You can completely remove your transformations by choosing Modify|Transform|Remove Transform. The shortcut keys are Shift+Cmd+Z or Shift+Ctrl+Z. You can also use the Edit|Undo command to remove your last action.

Repeatedly choosing Undo steps you back through previous commands until you run out of Undo levels. You can set the number of Undo levels in the Edit|Preferences|General dialog box. The program default is 100 Undo levels.

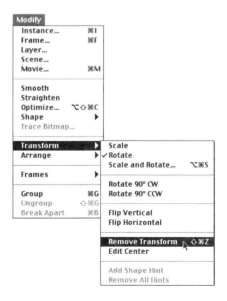

Moving and Reshaping Objects

You can move or reshape any selected object in Flash.

Moving by Hand

Once you select your object or objects, you can drag them anywhere in the image with the Arrow tool. You can move a fill and a stroke independently of each other.

Precise Positioning

You can move an object to a precise location in the image using the Info palette. Set the gadget box in the center of the palette to either the upper-left or the center coordinate. Then enter the new X and Y positions for the object. Press the Return/Enter key to "finalize" the move.

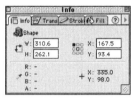

Simplifying Objects

Flash enables you to easily simplify curves or create hard edges.

Smoothing

Select the object using the Arrow tool. Then click the Smooth option on the Toolbox. With each click, the object gets smoother. You can see, from left to right, the original object, the object smoothed 3 times, and the object smoothed 40 times.

Straightening

Select the object using the Arrow tool. Then click the Straighten option on the Toolbox. With each click, the object gets less curved and more angular. You can see, from left to right, the original object, the object straightened two times, and the object straightened five times.

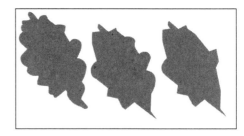

Editing with the Arrow Tool

You can use the Arrow tool to pull curves or corners from an object to change the object's shape. The object's fill (even if the object is also stroked) stretches or contracts to conform to the new shape.

1.

Choose the Arrow tool, but don't select any objects. Place your cursor at the edge of the object. If the Arrow tool cursor changes to an arrow with a curve, you can drag a curve away from the shape.

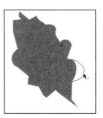

2.

Choose the Arrow tool, but don't select any objects. Place your cursor at the edge of the object. If the Arrow tool cursor changes to an arrow with a corner, you can drag a corner point away from the shape.

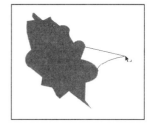

Editing as Bézier Points

Using the new Subselect tool and new Bézier Pen tool, you can directly edit any point on an object. You need to use the Subselect tool first to show the points.

Adding Points

Select the Pen tool. Place the cursor along the outline of the object. The cursor changes to a Pen with a plus sign to show it's OK to click to add a point. When you see the Pen Plus cursor, click to add the point. You can add a new point to a segment only between two curve points.

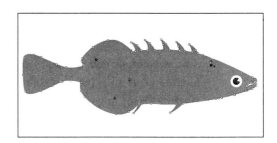

Changing Corner Points to Curves

Use the Subselect tool. Click a corner point to select it (it should become a solid square). Press and hold the Option/Alt key and drag the point to make it into a curve point.

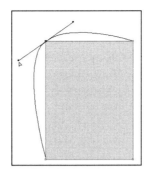

Changing Curve Points to Corners

Choose the Pen tool. Move your cursor on top of a corner point. The cursor shows a tiny caret. Click the curve point. It becomes a corner.

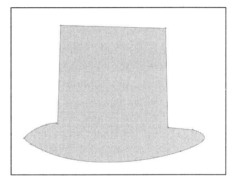

Reshaping a Curve Point to Create a Hard Bend

Choose the Subselect tool. Click to select a curve point. Press and hold the Opt/Alt key as you click a curve handle and drag it. You can now adjust each half of the tangent line individually.

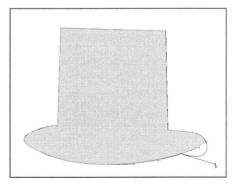

Deleting Points

The only kind of point that can be deleted is a corner point. Place the Pen tool on a corner point and click to remove it. To delete a curve point, first click it with the Pen tool to make it into a corner point.

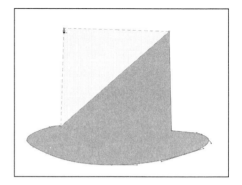

Reshaping Objects

You can reshape objects by dragging the Bézier handles or the control points.

1.

First, choose the Subselect tool. Click the outline to show the points. Click a specific point with the Subselect tool to show the associated Bézier handles. You'll see the handles of the point you clicked and the closer handles of the points on either side of the point selected.

2.

To move an anchor point, click it with the Subselect tool and drag it to another location.

3.

To reshape the curve by moving the tangent line, click and drag one of the ends of the tangent line. You can drag the tangent line up or down to deform the curve. This changes the shape of the curve without changing the length of the tangent line.

4.

You can make the curve deeper or more shallow by lengthening or shortening the tangent line.

When Objects Touch

Flash has an unusual cross between vector and raster drawing behaviors. Although the objects you draw in Flash are vectors, when they touch or overlap one another on the same layer, they act like raster (pixel-based) images. In other drawing programs, objects that overlap can be moved again so that they no longer overlap. Flash objects, however, interact with one another in some decidedly "non-vector" ways.

Same Colors Merge

When you drag one object on top of another object of the same color and then deselect the objects, the entire area occupied by the same color becomes one object. The two objects merge.

Different Colors Cut

When you drag one object on top of another object of a different color and then deselect the objects, the two objects don't merge. Instead, if you move the top object, it leaves a hole in the bottom object where the objects had overlapped.

Although this feature might seem like a flaw, this behavior makes it very easy to create new shapes.

Lines and Shapes Bisect

When you drag a line (created with the Pencil or Pen tool) on top of a shape, the line cuts holes in the shape. However, the shape also divides the line into smaller segments.

The Group

The unusual behavior of Flash drawing tools is an advantage when you want to create complex shapes, but it's not an advantage if you want to arrange multiple images in a single layer. Therefore, Flash gives you a way to rearrange objects so that they remain independent. It's called the Group.

Creating Groups

Select the object or objects you want to group. Choose Modify|Group from the top menu bar or press Cmd/Ctrl+G. You can group a single object so it won't combine or cut out any object it touches. You can also group already grouped objects to form a larger group.

Recognizing a Group

When you select a grouped object, it looks different. It has a thin rectangle as a bounding box. You can't set a new fill color or stroke color for a grouped object. You can't smooth or straighten a group, either.

Editing Groups

When you edit a group, you can manipulate the images that form that group as if they were individual objects again. You can change their location within the group, and you can add objects to the group.

1.

To edit a group, double-click it. On the Timeline, you'll see the group appear next to the current Scene or Timeline location.

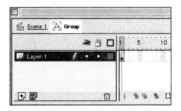

2.

The other objects on your monitor dim, and the group appears in front of them. If the group consists of individual objects, you can edit them now.

3.

To edit a group within a group, keep double-clicking until you see an individual object selected. Anything in front of the object in the main scene is hidden when you edit the object. The Timeline indicates how far down the group extends.

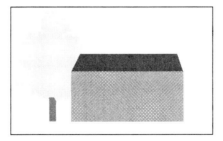

4.

To get out of Group Edit mode, click the Scene or Timeline level you wish to work in. You can also double-click a blank area of canvas to move one level up.

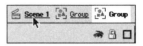

Stacking Order

You can change the stacking order of grouped elements to change the one on the top or bottom or to send groups lower or higher in the stack. Choose Modify|Arrange and select the option you want. If groups and shapes are on the same layer, all the shapes are on the bottom of the stack. You can't change the stacking order of ungrouped shapes.

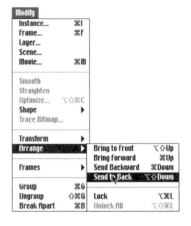

Ungrouping Groups

To ungroup a grouped object, choose Modify| Ungroup or press Shift+Cmd/Ctrl+G. You can completely remove the group and its elements from the image by pressing the Delete or Backspace key.

Importing Vector Images

Flash allows you to import images from vector programs like FreeHand or Illustrator. The imported images appear as grouped objects. You can easily import files from FreeHand, although complex effects might not translate well. Many Flash users like to build all their objects in FreeHand because the Bézier tool is easier to use and the program has more features for creating vector graphics. You can easily build entire sites in FreeHand 9 and import them into Flash for animation.

Importing Vector Graphics from FreeHand

Before you import a vector graphic, you need to prepare it first in your drawing program. Make sure that you use layers for anything that you want to import into its own layer.

1.

Choose File|Import and, in the dialog box that appears, locate the vector file you want. The Mac and Windows dialog boxes differ. On the Mac, double-click each file name to import or click once to select the file name and then click Add. When the list is complete, click Import. On Windows, you may choose multiple files by Ctrl+clicking the file name. Click Open to import the items.

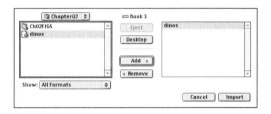

2.

If your image contains multiple pages, you can import each page as a scene or as a keyframe. You can import vector layers as Flash layers or keyframes, or flatten the image to a single layer. If you flatten the image, overlapping objects are treated with the normal Flash drawing behavior. You can import any page range of a multiple-page document.

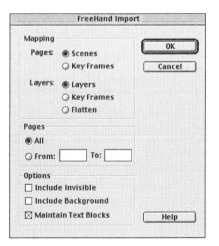

3.

Once you click the Import button, Flash imports the image into the current movie. If you have chosen to import layers, they appear in the Timeline. Each item is imported as a group.

Importing Vector Graphics from Adobe Illustrator

You can import either an .ai or an .eps file created in Adobe Illustrator 88 through Illustrator 6 formats. Each item appears as a group. To edit the imported document, ungroup the items or double-click the items until you reach the element to edit. If you want to ungroup overlapping items, move each item onto its own layer before ungrouping.

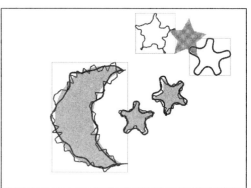

When you try to open an .ai or .eps image saved on the Mac, you might see a warning that the file has not imported completely. Allow the image to import anyway—it will usually be OK. The warning appears on both the Mac and Windows, but only on files created on the Mac. When in doubt, save your Illustrator file in Illustrator 88 format. It's the only one that doesn't produce errors.

Importing Raster Graphics

Flash can import a variety of raster (bitmapped) graphics formats, including JPG, GIF, and PNG files. The Import dialog box is the same one used for vector graphics. Although you cannot change individual pixels in Flash, you can edit the bitmapped files in Fireworks. You can convert bitmapped images to vector images or you can break them apart and use them as fills.

Importing Photoshop Files

To import a Photoshop file on either Windows or the Mac, you need to have QuickTime 4 installed. You'll see this message if QuickTime is on your system. If it isn't, you'll receive the message that one or more files were not imported because there were problems reading them.

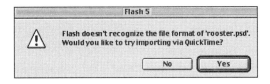

Converting Bitmapped Images to Vector Images

You can convert a bitmapped image to a vector graphic. You have complete control over the fidelity of the conversion, but if you have a complex image and don't want to simplify it, you might be better off leaving it as a raster graphic. You need to trade off time, quality, and file size.

1.

Select the bitmapped image. Choose Modify| Trace Bitmap.

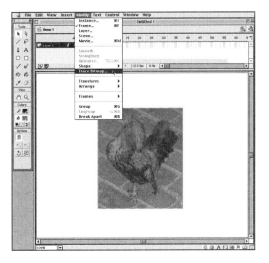

2.

In the Trace Bitmap dialog box, enter the desired Color Threshold. The smaller the setting, the more colors you'll get in your traced image. However, as you make the Color Threshold smaller, you'll significantly increase the amount of time needed to trace the bitmap, your RAM requirements, and final size of your movie. A setting of 10 is quite faithful to the original colors.

3.

Enter the desired Minimum Area size. This number controls the amount of detail in your tracing. The lower the number, the more detail that appears in your image (taking more time, RAM, and file size). The image on the top shows a minimum area of 20, while the image on the bottom shows a minimum area of 100. Both images use a Color Threshold of 50.

4.

Select a Curve Fit setting from the drop-down menu. This setting controls the jaggedness of the final shapes. Selecting Pixels gives you a tight, very jagged, and detailed result with many points. A Very Smooth setting gives the fewest jagged areas and the fewest possible points to define each shape.

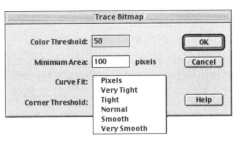

5.

Select a Corner Threshold setting from the drop-down menu to control sharp edges on the final shapes. You have a choice of Many Corners, Normal, or Few Corners. The image on the top has many corners; the one on the bottom has few corners. You can see the differences mainly in the hard edges around the outside of the image. The Many Corners setting keeps sharp points sharp, whereas the Few Corners changes most of them to curves.

6.

After you trace the bitmap, you can delete unneeded areas and manipulate the remaining shapes exactly as you would any other vector object in Flash.

Breaking Apart Bitmapped Images

The Break Apart command when used with bitmapped images (that have not been converted to vector objects), allows you to paint or fill with the bitmap. Breaking apart the image also allows you to erase part of it, which you can't do with a placed bitmap.

1.

Select the bitmapped image. Choose Modify| Break Apart.

2.

Click the broken-apart bitmapped image with the Eyedropper tool to use the bitmapped image as your current fill.

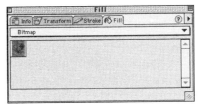

3.

You can use the Paintbrush tool to paint freeform shapes from the image.

4.

You can use a geometric shape with the bitmapped fill. If you transform either the original broken-apart bitmap or any piece filled with the broken-apart bitmap, you can sample it again with the Eyedropper tool and use the new image as a fill. Here, the bitmap was broken apart, skewed 45 degrees, and scaled to 33 percent of the original size. It was then used as a fill on the Ellipse tool.

Breaking Apart Text

You can also break apart text. When you do, you can reshape the letters as if they were normal vector objects and fill the letters with a gradient or bitmapped fill. After you have broken apart text, however, you can no longer edit it with the Text tool.

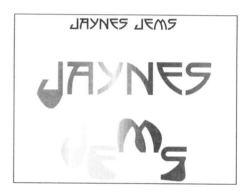

You can break apart only TrueType fonts. If you want to break apart a PostScript font, you need ATM (Adobe Type Manager) installed on your machine. Should you attempt to break apart a bitmapped font, it will disappear from the screen.

Chapter 3
Organizing Your Drawing

- Learn to create symbols

- Learn to create and share Libraries

- Learn about layers

By Sherry London

Creating Graphic Symbols

Whenever you use a graphic on a Web page, that graphic will be transferred from the Web server to the viewer's browser. This process takes time—sometimes, a lot of time. Fast-loading graphics are the *sine qua non* of the professional Web designer. They are the Holy Grail.

Flash helps create fast-loading graphics by allowing you to store a graphic that is used multiple times in a movie as a *symbol*. The symbol is stored once and can be used many times. You can change the color, size, orientation, and placement of the symbol, but all the instances (individual uses of a symbol) derive from the one downloaded shape.

The Greek philosopher Plato theorized that an "ideal form" exists for everything—a perfect chair, perhaps, that exists as an ideal from which all other chairs in the real world descend. Flash keeps the "perfect example" as a symbol from which you can derive many instances. You can store these symbols in a Library for each project, and you can share the Library (a feature new to Flash 5) among multiple developers across the many movies that might be combined to make up one Web site.

Graphic Symbols

You can create three different types of symbols in Flash: graphic symbols, button symbols, and movie clip symbols. A graphic symbol is either a static object or an animation that uses the Timeline of the main movie (see Chapter 4 for information on Timelines). You can create a graphic symbol using either the Convert To Symbol command or the New Symbol command.

Making a Graphic Symbol from an Existing Object

You can make a graphic symbol from an existing image by using the Insert|Convert To Symbol command.

1.

Select the object that you want to convert to a symbol. You can use any of the selection techniques described in Chapter 2.

2.

Choose Insert|Convert To Symbol or press F8 to execute the command.

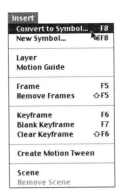

3.

The Symbol Properties dialog box appears. Choose the Graphic radio button. Then type whatever name you want for your symbol in the Name field of the dialog box.

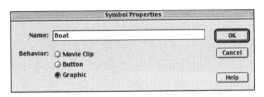

You should always take the time to name your symbols. Having a Library with 100 images each named "Symbol x" is a recipe for disaster.

4.

You know that your image is now a symbol because it is surrounded by a blue box. If you deselect the object, the blue box disappears, but it will reappear if you click the object with the Arrow tool again. When an image is a symbol, none of the editing tools will change the object. You need to enter Symbol Edit mode (discussed later in this chapter) in order to change the symbol.

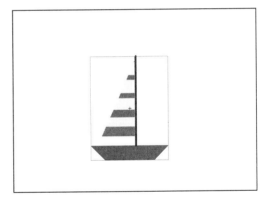

5.

If you choose Window|Library, you can see that the symbol has been added to your project library.

Creating a Graphic Symbol from Scratch

You can also use the drawing tools to create a symbol directly, but the procedure is different from creating an object.

1.

With nothing on the stage selected, choose Insert|New Symbol (Cmd/Ctrl+F8).

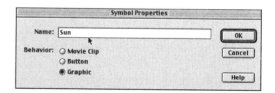

2.

The Symbol Properties dialog box appears again. Select the Graphic radio button. Name your symbol.

3.

You'll see a blank stage with a crosshair in the center. The crosshair marks the center point of your symbol. Notice the entry for your new symbol in the Library. Where did your original image go when you inserted the symbol? It's still there, but it isn't visible. At the top-left corner of the Timeline window, you can see an entry for Scene 1 (which was your image-in-progress) and for your symbol.

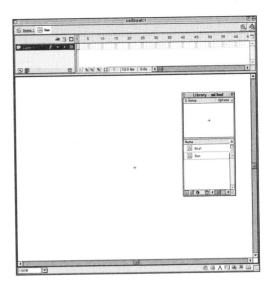

4.

Draw your symbol using any of the drawing tools. You may create more than one object to be part of the same symbol.

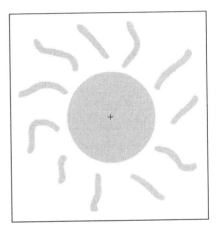

5.

When you're done creating the symbol, return to Scene 1 by clicking Scene 1 at the top-left corner of the Timeline window. You won't see your new symbol until you actually place it on the stage.

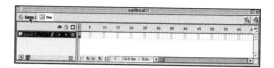

Button Symbols

Button symbols are used to create objects that respond to user clicks. When you create an element as a button, it acquires a 4-frame Timeline with an Up, Over, Down, and Hit state. You'll learn how to use button symbols in Chapter 7.

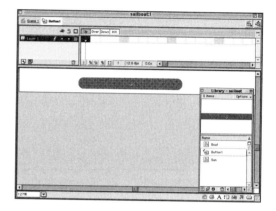

Movie Clip Symbols

Movie clip symbols are animations that contain their own Timeline. When you edit a movie clip symbol, you can see that the single-frame animation in the main Timeline contains the many frames of the movie clip itself. You'll learn more about movie clips and how to use them in Chapter 5.

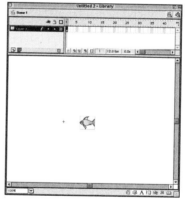

Using Symbols

Now that you know how to create symbols, it's time to look more carefully at how you use them.

Creating an Instance

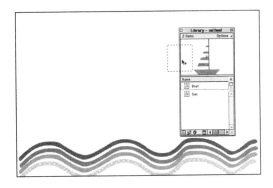

You cannot place the "real" symbol onto your movie. When you drag an object out of the Library palette, you are actually placing an instance of that symbol onto the stage. The symbol itself remains safely in place in the Library palette. Therefore, an *instance* is an example of a symbol that is located in a specific position on the stage. It is linked to the symbol. If you change the symbol to add a shape or alter a line, all the linked instances are automatically changed as well.

1.

Click the symbol in the Library that you want to place on the stage.

2.

Drag the instance onto the stage.

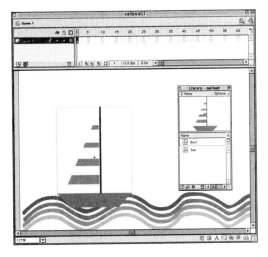

3.

If you're using the graphic instance in an animation, click the last frame in the Timeline in which you want the instance to be visible. Press F5 or choose Insert|Insert Frame. In the screenshot shown here, the instance is added to Frame 50.

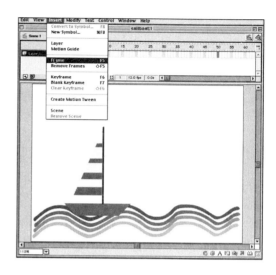

Manipulating Instances

You can change brightness, tint, or Alpha on instances using the Effect panel.

Brightness Effect

The Brightness effect makes the instance darker or lighter. You can apply a Brightness effect ranging from -100 to +100. Change the Effect type to Brightness in the Effect panel and drag the slider to the desired degree of brightness.

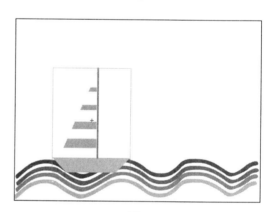

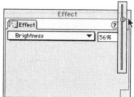

Tint Effect

You can change the color tint of an instance by applying the Tint effect.

1.

Change the effect type to Tint and select a color by clicking the color slider or by using the Tint Color picker. You can also enter the exact RGB values if you prefer.

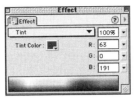

2.

Drag the slider next to the Tint's Alpha field (the top field on the right) to control how much of the chosen color tints the instance. If you select purple as your tint color, a 100 percent Alpha setting makes the entire instance a solid purple, but 20 percent Alpha gives the instance only a hint of purple.

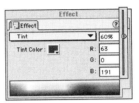

Alpha Effect

The Alpha effect controls the opacity of the instance. An Alpha setting of 100 percent is fully opaque and an Alpha setting of 0 percent is completely transparent. To apply the Alpha effect, change the effect type to Alpha and drag the slider next to the Alpha field to the desired level of transparency.

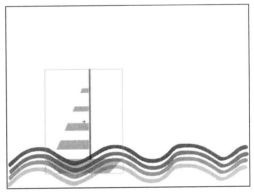

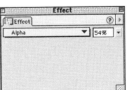

Advanced Effect

The Advanced effect uses a mathematical formula to adjust the colors in an instance. The columns on the left of the Advanced effect panel allow you to pick percentages of color values to adjust, while the right-hand columns assign a fixed value. For every color in the instance, the Advanced effect takes the original RGB color value, multiplies it by the percentage that you assign to the R, G, B, or Alpha component, and then adds the number on the right to get a final value for that color. You can create very subtle color changes with this effect.

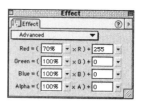

Getting Information About an Instance

You can find out information about any instance in your movie from the Info panel, the Instance panel, or the Movie Explorer.

Getting Information from the Info Panel

Select the instance and the look at the Info panel. You can see the width and height of the instance. You can also see the X,Y coordinates location. The black dot on the upper-left of the tiny bounding box icon in the Info panel indicates that the X,Y coordinates shown here are those of the upper-left corner of the instance. You can click the center dot on the icon in the Info panel to get the X,Y coordinates from the center.

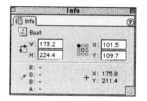

Getting Information from the Instance Panel

The Instance panel shows you the symbol from which the instance is derived. It also identifies the instance as a Graphic, a Button, or a Movie Clip and allows you to change its type. You can specify whether the instance loops, and you can view the starting frame in which the instance is visible. Opt/Alt+Double-clicking an instance brings the Instance panel to the front.

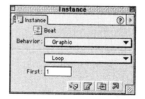

Getting Information from the Movie Explorer Panel

You can use the Movie Explorer panel to see which symbols and instances are used in a movie.

1.

Make the Movie Explorer panel visible by clicking the Movie Explorer icon at the bottom of the stage window or by selecting Movie Explorer from the Window menu.

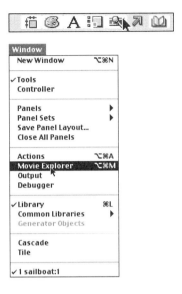

2.

The Movie Explorer panel shows you where the keyframes for each instance are located. Click an instance in a scene to see its location. The boat in Scene 1 has only a single keyframe defined. (A keyframe is a major reference point for an instance, and a location where you can make changes to opacity, scale, location, or rotation.)

3.

The Movie Explorer panel also shows each symbol used in the movie. Even though you might have multiple instances of a symbol in multiple keyframes in a scene, you see only one symbol entry.

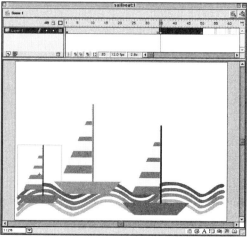

Editing Symbols and Instances

You can edit both symbols and instances of symbols. If you edit a symbol, you alter every instance of it. However, as you have seen, you can alter the position, size, or orientation of an instance or change its tint, brightness, or Alpha without changing the symbol itself.

Transforming Instances

With the Arrow tool, you can select a symbol instance and transform it by changing the height, width, size, or angle of rotation as you learned in Chapter 2. These changes affect only the instance—not the symbol itself.

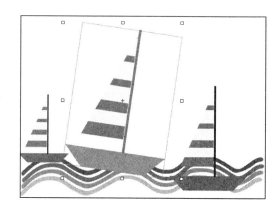

Symbol Editing Mode

In Symbol Editing mode, you can edit the symbol alone on the stage.

1.

Select an instance whose symbol you want to edit.

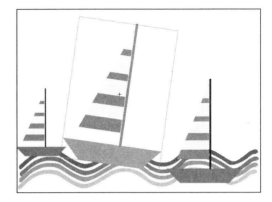

2.

Choose Edit Symbols from the Edit menu or press Cmd/Ctrl+E. You can also enter Symbol Editing mode by double-clicking the symbol in the preview pane of the Library.

3.

Make any changes you want to the symbol. Here, I added stripes to the sail and then added a smaller sail next to the large one.

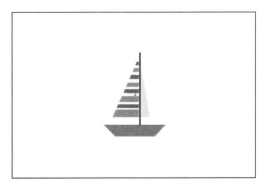

4.

Return to the movie by selecting Edit|Edit Movie (Cmd/Ctrl+E) or by clicking Scene 1 at the top-left of the Timeline. You can see that all instances of the symbol have been changed.

Edit In Place

Edit In Place allows you to view the symbol in context as you make changes.

1.

Double-click an instance of a symbol on the stage. Everything else on the stage fades and only the instance you click stays bright.

2.

Make your editing changes. Notice that all other instances of the same symbol update simultaneously. Return to Movie Edit mode when you are finished.

3.

Another way to return to Movie Edit mode is to choose the scene to edit from the Edit Scene button at the top-right of the Timeline.

Edit In New Window

You can also edit the symbol in a new window if you prefer. The advantage is that you can see both the movie and your symbol at the same time. Select the symbol instance to edit. Ctrl+Right-click the selected instance and choose Edit In New Window from the pop-up menu. Change the symbol and return to the movie as in the other symbol editing methods.

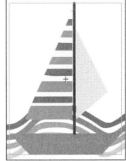

Replacing Symbols

You can swap one symbol for another for a single instance. The new symbol replaces the original but keeps all of the properties, effects, and keyframes assigned to the original instance.

1.

Select the instance that you want to replace.

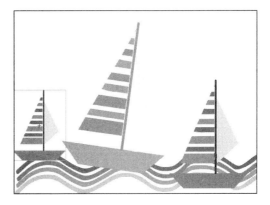

2.

Click the Swap Symbol icon at the bottom of the Instance panel.

3.

Select the new symbol in the Swap Symbol dialog box. You will see all the symbols currently in the Library.

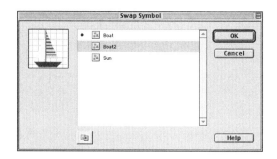

4.

When you click OK in the Swap Symbol dialog box, you'll see the new symbol in your drawing.

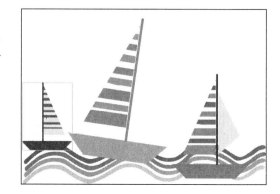

Breaking Apart

You can sever the link between the instance and the symbol by choosing Modify|Break Apart. The selected instance becomes an ungrouped collection of objects that can be edited individually. As ungrouped objects, their stacking order drops to the lowest levels of the layer. They also lose any transformations applied via the Effect panel. If the objects are completely ungrouped, they will combine with each other as do other ungrouped Flash graphics.

Storing Symbols

All the symbols for your movie are stored in the Project Library. You have a great deal of control over the arrangement and organization of the objects in the Project Library. You can also share the Project Library among movies.

The Project Library

The Project Library stores all the image assets and code assets for a project. Each type of asset has its own symbol. You can also arrange the contents of the Library to suit yourself.

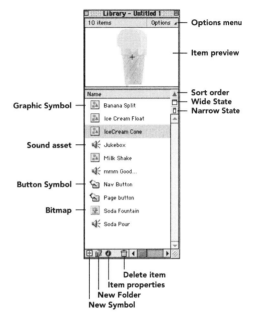

Seeing Library Details

Click the Wide State icon on the right side of the Library panel to show all the details in the Library. Click the Narrow State icon to reduce the size of the Library panel to hide the details. You can sort the Library items by clicking any column head in Wide State view and change the sort order from high to low by clicking the Sort Order icon on the right side of the Library window.

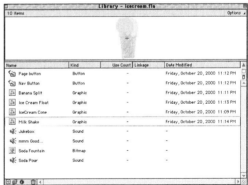

Using Folders

You can add folders to your Library and then move items into the folder for storage. Using folders saves space when you view the Library and allows you to organize your movie assets into logical groups.

1.

Click the New Folder icon at the bottom of the Library panel. An untitled folder icon appears in the Library panel.

2.

Enter a name for the folder. Press the Return/ Enter key to "register" the folder name.

3.

Drag any assets in the Library into the folder.

4.

Choose Collapse All Folders from the Options menu on the Library panel to view only the folders and not their contents. You can also double-click a folder to collapse it if it is open or expand it if it is not.

Nesting Folders

You can store folders inside folders. In the example shown, the Static Graphic Assets folder stores folders containing both the bitmapped images and the graphic symbols in the movie.

Using and Sharing Libraries

A new feature in Flash 5 is the ability to create shared Libraries. To share a Library, you define an item as shared in the Library associated with the movie in which it is created. Once you publish that movie on the Web, other movies can link to that shared Library and use its assets. Using a shared Library, you can link to an asset without making it part of the movie. You can also link multiple movies to the same set of common elements to save on file size. The item is downloaded as soon as the first instance in which it is used appears in a movie.

Creating a Linkable Item

Choose Linkage from the Library Options menu or Ctrl+Right-click the asset name in the Library panel. Choose the Export This Symbol radio button and give the asset an identifying name that contains no spaces. Click OK to exit the dialog box. To share every item in the Library, repeat this process for each Library item.

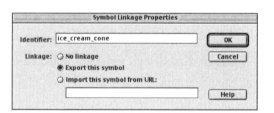

Publishing a Shared Library

To publish a shared Library, you need to assign a URL to it. Choose Shared Library Properties from the Library panel Options menu. Type in the URL. Click OK to close the dialog box.

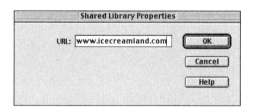

Using Shared Assets

To use a shared Library in a movie, you need to first save the movie that contains the Library that you want to share. In a new movie, choose File|Open As Shared Library and select the desired Library. Drag the assets that you want to use into the Library for the new movie or drag them onto the stage.

You don't need to have an .swf file to use the assets of a shared Library, but you need to publish the shared Library before you can test the movie that uses its assets.

File	
New	⌘N
Open...	⌘O
Open as Library...	⇧⌘O
Open as Shared Library...	
Close	⌘W
Save	⌘S
Save As...	⇧⌘S
Revert	
Import...	⌘R
Export Movie...	⌥⇧⌘S
Export Image...	
Publish Settings...	⇧⌘F12
Publish Preview	▶
Publish	⇧F12
Page Setup...	
Print Margins...	
Print Preview	
Print...	⌘P
1 IceCreamWars	
2 icecream.fla	
3 flower	
Quit	⌘Q

Using Layers

Layers provide another way to help you organize your movies. If you have used layers in Photoshop, Illustrator, FreeHand, or a page layout program, the concept should be familiar to you. Each layer is independent of the other layers, and each can be animated separately and its stacking order changed. Graphical items on a layer don't interact with items on another layer, so if you place a tree in Layer 1 and a bird on top of that tree in Layer 2, the bird won't cut a hole out of the tree—even if both objects are simple shapes.

In general, you will want to use layers as much as possible and keep only one item on a layer unless you plan to animate the entire layer as a unit. You will also want to create separate layers for sound files, comments, actions, and labels to make them easier to identify. You can have "normal" layers, guide layers and mask layers. You'll learn about guide and mask layers in Chapters 4 and 5.

Creating Layers

To create a layer, click the Insert Layer icon at the bottom left of the Layers list in the Timeline window. An unnamed layer is added to your movie. You can rename the layer by double-clicking the layer name and entering a new name for the layer.

Hiding, Showing, Locking, and Outlining Layers

Using the icon symbols in the Layers list, you can hide, lock, or display layers as outlines.

1. You can hide a layer by clicking the Eye column for that layer. Clicking the Eye column on a hidden layer makes it visible again.

2. You can lock layers so that the items they contain cannot be moved or edited.

3. Clicking the Display As Outlines column changes the items on that layer to outlines in the color shown on the layers list. This feature enables you to see quickly which items are on that layer.

4. This layer is both the Active layer (because it is highlighted) and outlined.

5. This layer is hidden, so you can't see what's on it.

6. This layer is locked.

7. Add layers by clicking the Insert Layer icon.

8. Add a Guide layer by clicking the Add Guide Layer icon.

Cutting and Pasting

After you add a new layer, you can draw or create content on that layer. You can also cut objects out of an existing layer. After you select the object to move to a new layer, choose Edit|Cut. Then create the new layer or make an existing layer active. Choose Edit|Paste In Place to put the cut object in the same spot on the new layer.

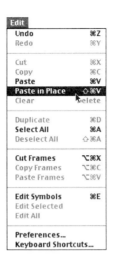

Reordering Layers

You can change the order of a layer by dragging it into a new position. Because the ice cream soda could not possibly be behind the banana split as shown here, you can drag its layer to the top of the Layer list. The item at the top of the list appears on top of overlapped items in the movie. The elements on the layer at the bottom of the list appear behind the other objects in the movie.

Before

After

Chapter 4
So You Want to Be Disney

- Learn how to use the Timeline

- Create cel animations with onion skinning

- Create motion tweens

- Create motion guides

- Assemble shape tweens

By Sherry London

Timeline and Animation Basics

The Timeline is the most important work area when you create an animation. The purpose of the Timeline is to show movement over time. All the movement in the movie is choreographed from the Timeline.

Meet the Timeline

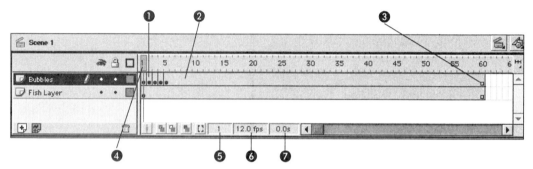

1. *Keyframe*—A keyframe marks the point at which a change occurs in an animation. You need to create a keyframe wherever you want a change to occur.

2. *Empty Frame*—The frame is the basic unit on the Timeline. All activity happens in a frame. In an empty frame, however, no changes occur. You typically create an empty frame to tell Flash how long to show a layer.

3. *Blank Keyframe*—No change occurs in a blank keyframe. However, tweening sequences occur between two keyframes. You need to set a blank ending keyframe before you can create a tween. The blank keyframe shown here marks the end of the Timeline sequence for this layer.

4. *Playhead*—The playhead tracks the display time of your animation. It shows which frame is displayed at a specific time in the animation.

5. *Current Frame indicator*—This reports which frame the playhead is currently displaying. This is an information-only field that cannot be changed.

6. *Frame Rate indicator*—This shows the number of frames that will be displayed per second. 12 fps is the "standard" Flash frame rate for Web-delivered animations. This is an information-only field.

7. *Elapsed Time indicator*—This shows the elapsed time from the first frame to the current frame being displayed. This is an information-only field.

Animation Types

Flash enables you to create two types of animations: cel and tweened. In cel animations, you create a new keyframe every frame or so. Tweened animations are animations for which Flash computes either the motion or the shape of the changes. On this image, the top layer (Fish2) is a tweened animation, as you can see from the line running through the frames, and the middle layer (Bubbles) is a cel animation with only five keyframes. The Fish layer is static.

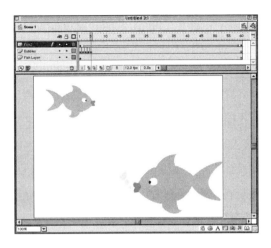

Traditional Animation

Traditional animation of the type produced by Walt Disney and the other cartoon animation houses is called cel animation. Each cel was painted by an artist and layered over a static background. The artist created the walks, runs, or other motion needed and these cels (the equivalent of a digital keyframe) were outlined, inked, and then photographed to create the motion. The artists were really the "actors" in the cartoons, and their skills conveyed the drama in the scene. Let's take a brief look at how traditional animation works and learn how to create cel-based animation in Flash.

Principles of Animation

Traditional animation depends on the principles of squash, stretch, and anticipation to provide the dramatic aspects of the scene.

Squash

An animated figure squashes up quite small when it hits a wall. This change dramatically conveys halted motion.

Stretch

When an animated object falls quickly or is pulled up with extreme force, it visually stretches to show this force applied.

Anticipation

An object shows anticipation when it turns left before moving right or leans steeply as it comes to a screeching halt before running into an obstacle. This motion is very natural motion, and the cartoon simply exaggerates this human reaction.

Creating a Cel-Based Animation

In a cel-based animation in Flash, you create a keyframe in every frame and make changes in the action of every frame.

1.

Create your starting static images in the first frame of the Timeline.

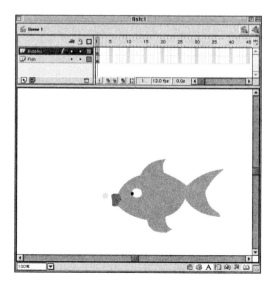

2.

Select the last frame in all the layers by clicking inside each layer's final frame with the Shift key pressed. Then choose Insert|Frame (F5). This marks the duration of the animation.

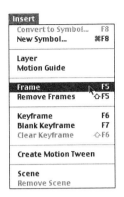

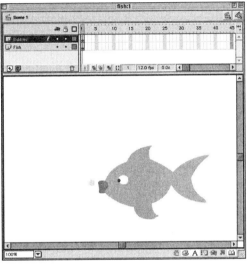

3.

Move the playhead to Frame 2. Choose Insert Keyframe (F6).

4.

Move or change an object (make it bigger, change its location, etc.). In this example, the bubble gets a little bit bigger and moves up.

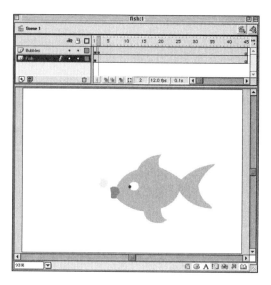

5.

Continue to insert keyframes and alter the elements on the animation layer. You can add objects and move them around in any way you please.

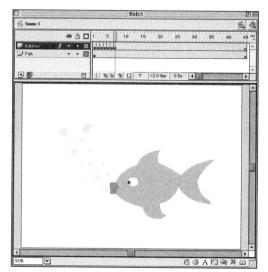

Previewing the Animation

You can preview this simple animation in two ways: you can play the movie or you can scrub the frames.

Playing a Movie

Press the Return/Enter key or choose Control|Play to run the animation. You will see all the frames in a simple cel animation. However, when you begin to build more complex animations with masks, this technique won't work. You'll need to use the Test Movie command in the Control menu instead. Test Movie actually builds a movie file and previews it using the Flash Player; the Play command simply runs through all the frames.

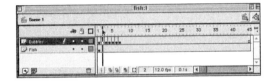

Scrubbing the Playhead

When you *scrub* the movie, you move the playhead back and forth through the frames manually to preview the animation. Scrubbing is very helpful when you build an animation.

Onion Skinning

When traditional animators create sequential movements, they typically draw on a pad of tracing paper so that they can see what the last drawing was. Seeing the last pose makes drawing the continuing action much easier. Flash provides the digital equivalent, which is called *onion skinning*. You set the number of frames to show at one time and you can "see through" these frames to see where you've been and where you need to go. The frame under the playhead is shown in full color—the frames that are onion skinned are dimmed. You can edit only the frame under the playhead.

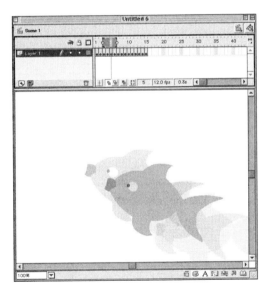

The Onion Skin feature shows onion skin for all visible layers. Turn off the eye on the layers that you don't want to onion skin. Otherwise, you can get very confused.

Turning on Onion Skinning

Turn on the Onion Skin feature by clicking the first Onion Skin icon at the bottom of the Timeline window.

Using Onion Skin Outlines

You might find it easier to see the separate sheets of onion skin if you change the onion skin display so that it shows outlines of objects. Click the Onion Skin Outlines icon (the second of the set of Onion Skin icons) at the bottom of the Timeline to show outlines only.

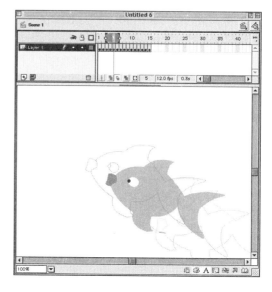

Setting Onion Skin Markers

You can determine how many frames on either side of the playhead you want to view as onion skin. When you click the Onion Skin button, the onion skin markers appear above the Timeline. Each end is indicated by a small circle and the range is indicated by dark gray shading. You can change that range by dragging the circle markers at either end of the range.

Changing Onion Skin Options

You can change the way the onion skin feature works. Click the Modify Onion Markers icon at the bottom of the Timeline. You can decide to always show the onion skin markers. You can also choose to make the onion skin range stay at a particular range of frames by choosing Anchor Onion (normally, the range moves with the playhead). You also have three automatic options for onion skin ranges: Onion 2, Onion 5, or Onion All.

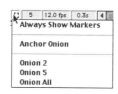

Editing Multiple Frames

Although the Onion Skin feature usually lets you edit only the frame under the playhead, by selecting the Edit Multiple Frames icon (the third of the onion skin icons at the bottom of the Timeline), you can edit any frame in the onion skin range just by clicking it.

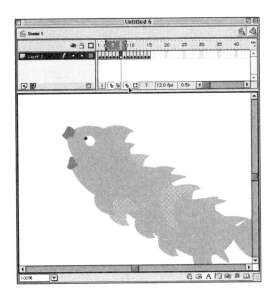

If you plan to use the Edit Multiple Frames option, make sure that your objects are all either symbols or groups, because it is difficult to select all of a multiple-part object when parts of it are covered up by onion skin from other frames.

Seeing Where You Are Going

When you create an animation, an excellent technique is to set the starting and ending keyframes first. The ending keyframe is perhaps the most important one. Once you know where you want to end, you can work toward a specific goal. Setting the ending onion skin marker to display the last frame of the animation gives you an image to work toward.

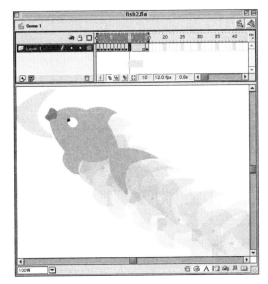

Motion Tweening

Flash gives you a way to avoid frame-by-frame animations. Motion tweens enable you to move your object from starting to ending position using only several mouse clicks to create the entire range of frames. The advantage of motion tweening for Web animations is that Flash saves only the start and end frames and calculates the frames between, or *tweens*, which results in a much smaller animation.

Creating the Motion Tween

You can create motion tweens with instances of a symbol, with groups, and with text. You can change the size, rotation, color, or Alpha of objects that are motion tweened.

1.

Drag or create an instance, a group, or a type object on the stage.

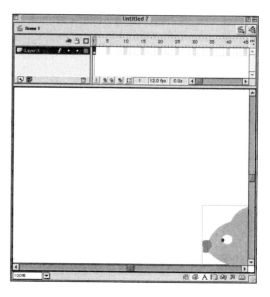

2.

Click inside the ending frame to select it and choose Insert|Frame (F5).

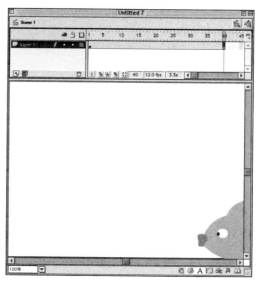

3.

Choose Insert|Create Motion Tween. You'll see an incomplete tween (indicated by dotted lines across the range of frames in the Timeline).

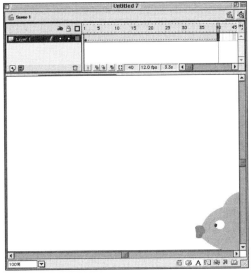

4.

With the playhead still at the ending keyframe, move the object to the ending position on the stage. The motion tween line automatically fixes itself and shows a solid line with an arrow at the end.

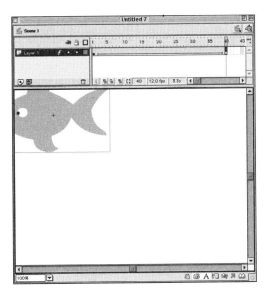

Making Multiple Motion Tweens

The motion tween occurs between the starting and ending points. You can create intermediate tweens by setting keyframes within the motion tween range.

1.

Scrub the playhead or turn on onion skinning to show the range of motion for the tween. Determine the frame that you want to change.

If you onion skin a motion tween, only the starting and ending frames are editable.

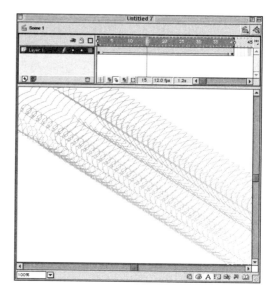

2.

Turn off onion skinning if it is on. Move the playhead to the frame where you want the motion to change. Move the object to the desired location on the stage. You'll see two motion tweens in the Timeline instead of one. (You can also preview the animation by turning on onion skining again.)

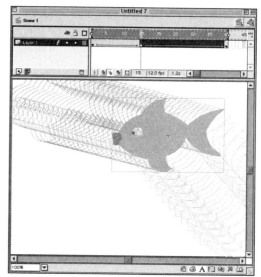

3.

If you don't like the location of the changed keyframe in the motion tween, you can move the keyframe in the Timeline by simply dragging it to a new frame. The motion tween repairs itself and changes to the new keyframe location.

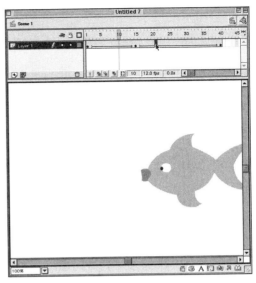

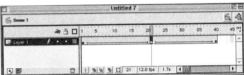

Motion Tween Options

You can tween attributes other than motion in a motion tween. You make some of the changes in the Frame panel and others using just the normal Flash tools.

Tweening Colors

When you apply the Tint Effect to keyframes in the motion tween, your Tint (or any other effect) will change from no effect to the full effect at the keyframe where you assigned the Tint or other effect. Move the playhead to the frame where you want the color change to occur. Select the object and then apply the desired effect.

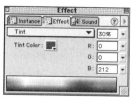

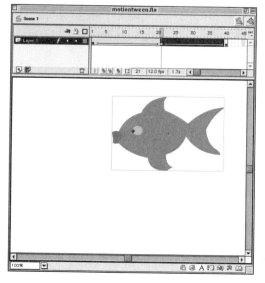

Scaling a Tween

To change the size of the object in a motion tween, set the playhead to the starting frame of the tween, select the object, and use the Scale option on the Arrow tool to resize the object. Move the playhead either to the ending frame or to the keyframe where the last size change should occur. Again, select the object and use the Scale option on the Arrow tool to change the object size.

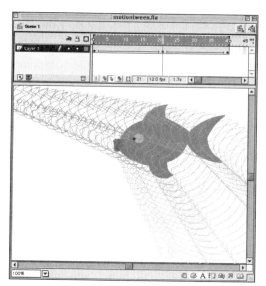

Rotational Effects

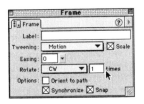

At the Frame panel, you specify the tweening method for a frame and set a rotation. You can rotate the object clockwise or counterclockwise. If you have already rotated the object using the Arrow tool, any rotation you specify in the Frame panel is added to the previous amount. Before you make any changes to the Frame panel, you must first select the object. When you apply a rotation, make sure that the playhead is on the first frame of the motion tween.

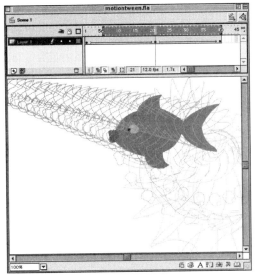

Fade In, Fade Out

You can make objects seem to fade in or fade out by applying an Alpha effect to a motion tween. For example, you could make buttons grow and increase in opacity as they twirl across the screen before landing in the correct spot on the Web page. Apply the Alpha effect at 0 percent to your starting frame and end the motion tween at 100 percent Alpha. To set intermediate changes that aren't linear, you can add keyframes.

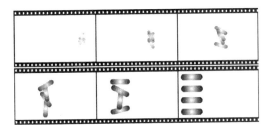

Setting Ease In and Ease Out

You can't really set a speed for your motion tween, but you can make it appear as if part of the tween (the start or the end) moves faster than the rest of the tween by setting the Easing slider in the Frame palette. At 0, no ease is applied to the image and every frame is the same distance apart. With Ease Out set to 100, you can see the gaps at the start of the motion tween. These gaps make it look as if the fish is moving much faster at the start of the tween than at the end of the tween. Easing in reverses the motion and makes the tween pick up speed as it ends.

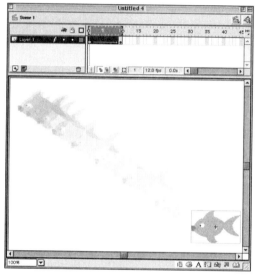

Tween Along a Path

You can create a tween that follows an independent path as it moves across the image.

1.

Create a new layer and add a motion tween to the object in the layer.

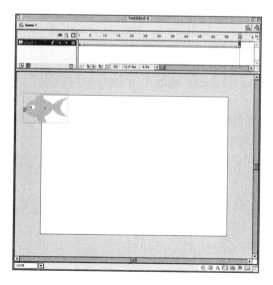

2.

Set the playhead to the start of the motion tween. Select the layer with the motion tween. Click on the Add Guide Layer icon at the bottom of the layers list. The new guide layer appears on top of the original layer. An arch symbol appears at the start of the guide layer.

3.

Use the Pencil tool to draw a path of any shape on the guide layer.

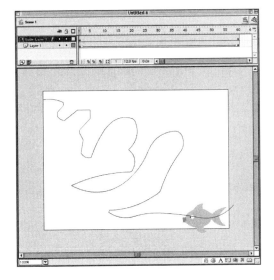

4.

Choose View|Snap To Objects to turn on the snapping feature.

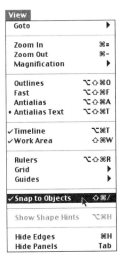

5.

Make sure that the playhead is at the first frame of the motion tween. Activate the guided layer. Select the object on the guided layer and drag it until it snaps to the path where you want the motion to begin.

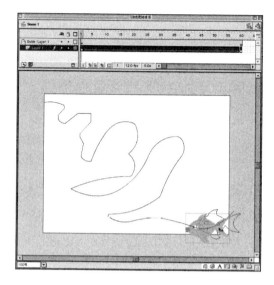

6.

Make sure that the playhead is at the last frame of the motion tween. Activate the guided layer. Select the object on the guided layer and drag it until it snaps to the path where you want the motion to end.

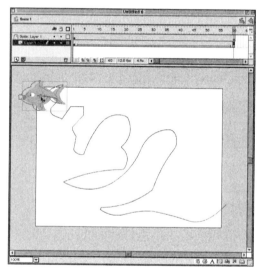

7.

You can make the guided object orient itself to the path (so that the fish changes direction as it swims, for example). Move the playhead to the start of the motion tween. Select the object. In the Frame panel check the Orient To Path checkbox.

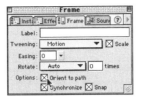

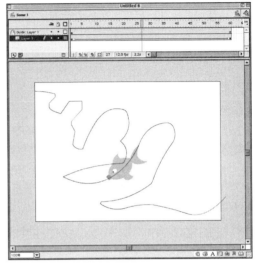

Attaching Multiple Layers to the Same Path

You can attach more than one layer to the same path. Create a new layer below the guide layer in the layer list. If some layers aren't guided, place the new layer above the non-guided layers but below the guide layer. Move the playhead so that it is no longer on the starting frame of the first guided layer. Insert a keyframe. Now drag the object and create a motion tween that ends later than the last frame of the first guided layer. Snap the object to the motion guide as you did for the first guided layer.

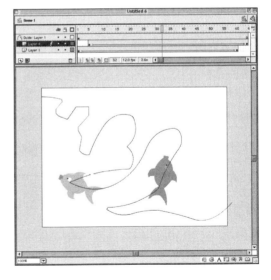

You can create the extra frames you need on the guide layer by selecting the frame that matches the last frame in the new guided layer and choosing Insert|Frame.

Shape Tweens

A shape tween is similar to a motion tween in that a change occurs between two frames. However, in a shape tween, you are actually changing one object into another. Another term for shape tween is *morph*. A motion tween requires a symbol, text, or a group, but in a shape tween, you cannot use a symbol, group, text block, or bitmap. You can, however, tween color, size, and location in either a shape or a motion tween.

Creating Simple Shape Tweens

Creating a shape tween is a bit different from creating a motion tween.

1.

Create a new layer for your shape tween and create a keyframe where you want the tween to begin. Create or import an object to be tweened. You can use only an ungrouped shape.

The two graphics shown in this part of the chapter are from the Ultimate Symbol Design Elements collection of demo images. You can find this set of demo images at **www.ultimatesymbol.com**. *Ultimate Symbol makes my favorite set of clip art. Because of the iconic nature of their symbols, they fit with almost anything, and the simple shapes work beautifully in Flash.*

2.

Select the ending frame for the shape tween and add a keyframe to it.

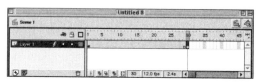

3.

Drag the playhead back to the first frame of the shape tween. Select the object. In the Frame panel, change the Tweening value to Shape. Set Blend to Distributive unless you are creating a shape tween that depends on straight lines, in which case you use the Angular blend method. Your shape tween range appears in the Timeline with light green shading (when you deselect the tween).

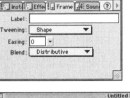

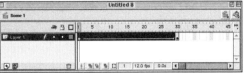

4.

Move the playhead to the last frame in the tween. Remove the starting image and draw or import the image for the end of the shape tween.

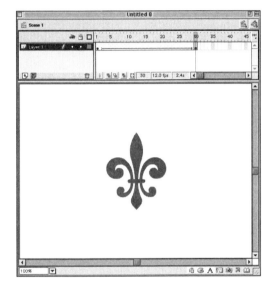

5.

Press the Return/Enter key to preview the shape tween or scrub the playhead. As you can see, the transition between these shapes is a bit rough. You can make the transition much better by using Shape Hints.

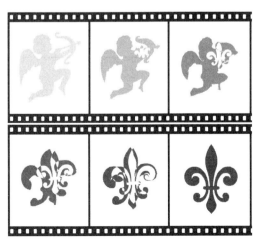

Shape Hints

When you create a shape tween between shapes that are extremely different, Flash has trouble deciding how to construct the in-between frames. You can help it make better decisions by adding Shape Hints. You must create your shape tween before you can add the hints, however. Shape Hints work by matching lettered circles at the critical points of the starting and ending images. By matching the starting letter *a* to the ending letter *a*, Flash can generate a much better tween.

1.

Once you've created a shape tween, set the playhead back to the first frame and choose Modify|Transform|Add Shape Hint. Flash adds a red circle with the letter *a* inside to the center of the starting shape.

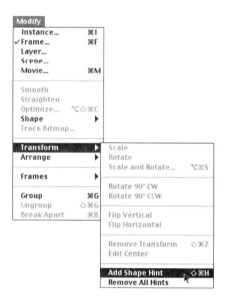

2.

Drag the circle to the first point that you want to identify. Macromedia suggests starting in the upper-left corner of the shape. If the shape has no upper-left corner, the top-center location will do.

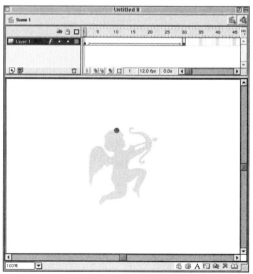

3.

Drag the playhead to the last frame of the shape tween. You'll see a red circle with the letter *a* inside in the center of the ending shape. Drag the circled letter to the upper-left or top-center point that corresponds to the point on the first shape where you placed your hint. The circled letter should turn green.

Flash adds a red circle when you first establish a Shape Hint. After you have placed the Shape Hint, the starting circle turns yellow and the ending one turns green.

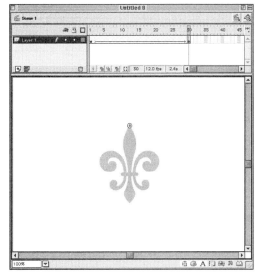

4.

Scrub the playhead to preview the animation. You should see a definite change. The change might not be enough, but the tween should look much better than it did before.

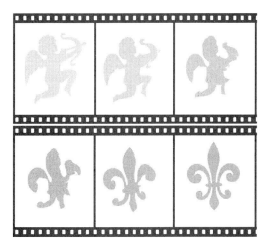

5.

You can continue to add Shape Hints to the starting image and place them at the corresponding locations on the ending image. Macromedia states that you will get the best results by placing the hints counterclockwise from the top-left of the image.

A very fast and convenient way to place Shape Hints is to use the keyboard shortcut Shift+Cmd/Ctrl+H. Place the hints one at a time and set the end point before you create a new hint.

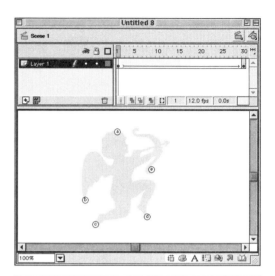

6.

Scrub the playhead or press the Return/Enter key to preview the animation.

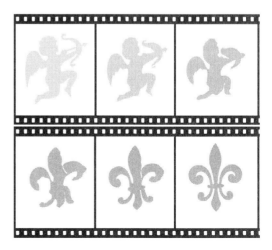

Multiple Shape Tweens

You can create additional shape tweens on the same layer, but you will keep things much simpler if you apply a shape tween to only one element on a layer at a time. To make the next shape tween, add the keyframe on the new ending frame, add your object, and set up the tween by selecting Shape from the Frame panel. When you go to the starting frame of the second tween to add Shape Hints, your original ending hints will be there. When you add a new hint, it will start with letter *a* again. You may drag it over the original ending letter *a* if you want. Set all your Shape Hints and preview the results.

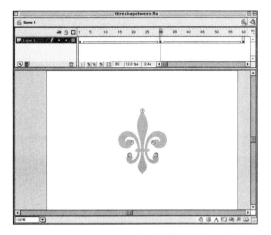

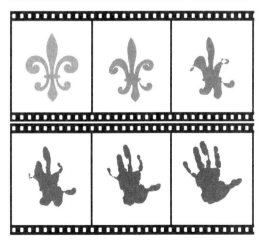

Chapter 5
Creating Complex Animations

- Learn how to create and use movie clips

- Learn about masks and how to use them

- Learn how to create frame labels and named instances on the Timeline

- Create scenes within your movies

- Learn how to load and unload movies

By Sherry London

Animating Animations

You can store entire animations as symbols. When you do, the Timeline of the symbol is stored as well. Making animation sequences into symbols allows you to use the symbols as part of a shared Library, which saves time if you want to use an animation sequence more than once. You can store animations in all three types of symbols: graphic, button, and movie clip. You'll learn about button symbols in Chapter 7.

Using Animated Graphic Symbols

When you create an animation and save it as a graphic symbol, the symbol uses the same Timeline as the main animation. The advantage of creating an animated graphic symbol, besides its reusability, is your ability to animate an animation. You can easily place multiple copies of an animation, tween the animation along a path, add color effects, or add size and angle transforms to it.

1.

Create your animation as usual. This static clock has an hour hand that rotates once in the animation and a minute hand that rotates 12 times during the same period.

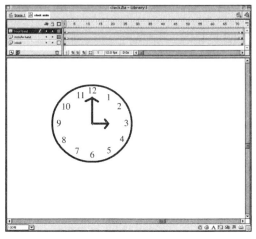

2.

Place your cursor at the top-left frame in the Timeline and click and hold (Mac) or right-click (Windows) to drop down a context menu. Choose Select All from the drop-down menu to select all the Timeline and the images on the stage.

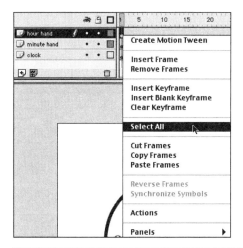

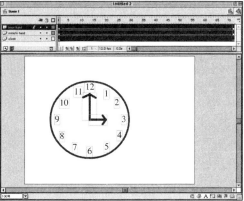

3.

With everything selected, place your cursor at the top-left frame in the Timeline and click and hold (Mac) or right-click (Windows) to drop down the context menu again. Choose Copy Frames from the menu.

You can also choose Cut Frames and save yourself a step, but until you've tried this procedure several times, it's safer not to cut the frames until you've created your symbol.

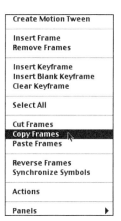

4.

Choose Insert|New Symbol.

The option Convert To Symbol should also be available. Though this option looks like a shorter process, don't do it. Your animation is likely not to work properly.

5.

In the dialog box, name your symbol and make it a graphic symbol. You'll see a blank stage with the center point of the new symbol marked with a cross.

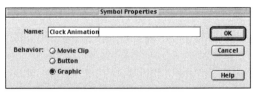

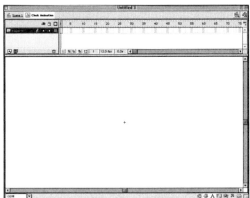

6.

Select the first frame in the Timeline. Choose Edit|Paste Frames.

When you paste the animation into a symbol, you need to center the animation on the center cross of the symbol editing window. If you don't manage to paste the animation so that it is centered, you may see unexpected results when you use the symbol. The clock, for example, is static as the hands move, and the hands stay centered. Therefore, the symbol must be centered as well. If the animation is not centered, keep trying until you get it to paste into the center. If necessary, you can go back to the main Timeline and add a different symbol. You could even create a new movie and add the symbol to that. You must get that symbol centered by pasting it. If you drag the animation to the center, you drag only the starting frame—you would need to readjust the center for every keyframe in the symbol. If the animation moves from side to side on the stage, you need to make sure that the pasted location matches the starting location of the animation when you created it on the stage.

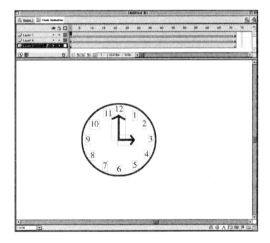

7.

Return to the main movie Timeline by clicking on the Scene 1 icon in the upper-left corner of the Timeline.

8.

Select all of the movie as you did in Step 2 and select Insert|Remove Frames. You're left with an empty movie, but the animation is in the Library for the movie. Unfortunately, the layers from the original clock animation remain in the movie and aren't deleted when the objects are removed.

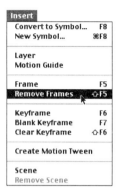

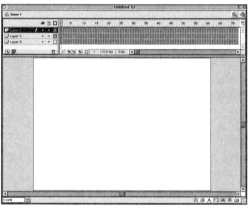

9.

Delete two of the three remaining layers by selecting the layer and clicking the Trashcan icon at the bottom of the Timeline layers list.

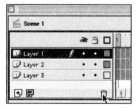

10.

Create a new layer and drag the graphic symbol animation for the movie from the Library back onto the stage.

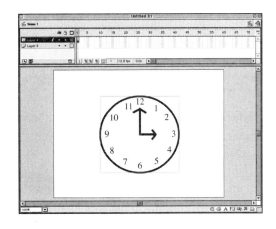

It would make much more sense to reuse the one layer still in the movie. However, you usually cannot drag the symbol onto it—the symbol flies back. Although adding frames to the layer and dragging the symbol back does work, I find it easier to add a clean new layer and then delete the layer that had been part of the original animation.

11.

If you want the animation in the graphic symbol to actually *play* in the movie, you need to add frames to the Timeline. If you want the entire animation to play, you need to add as many frames to the scene's Timeline as there are frames in the animation symbol. If you add fewer frames, less of the animation plays. To add frames, select the desired ending frame on the Timeline and press F5 or choose Insert|Frame.

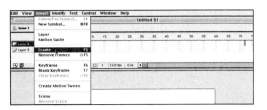

12.

For each instance of the graphic symbol animation you use, you can choose the starting frame and the looping behavior. Select the instance in Frame 1 and set both items in the Instance panel. The looping behavior really matters only if the movie has more frames than the graphic symbol. Your choices are Loop, Play Once, or Single Frame. In the example shown here, each clock has a different starting frame.

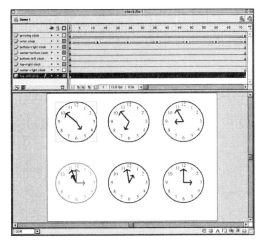

Single Frame is an exception. It displays only the selected frame number regardless of the number of frames the animation contains.

Using Movie Clips

A movie clip is a "super graphics symbol." It's the equivalent of packing an entire movie into a symbol. Where the graphic symbol uses the main movie's Timeline, the movie clip plays an entire animation inside a single frame in the main movie Timeline using its own Timeline. You can create an instance name for a movie clip, but not for a graphic symbol. Because you can name an instance in a movie clip, you can make the movie clip interactive—you can create a button to start or stop it, and you can refer to it in a script. However, to include either animation or interactivity in a movie clip, you need to use the Test Movie or Test Scene command; you can't see either one when you preview the movie or scrub the playhead.

You can view limited button activity if you select Control|Play Simple Buttons. However, you need to keep toggling this control on and off to be able to edit your animation.

Building a Movie Clip

To build a movie clip, follow the same process you used to create a graphic symbol animation, except choose Movie Clip as the Behavior in the Symbol Properties dialog box. You can either create the entire movie clip and copy it to a movie clip symbol or create a new symbol and develop the movie clip directly within the symbol's Timeline.

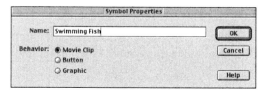

Scaling Movie Clips

If you create a movie clip and scale it, everything in the movie clip is scaled as well. If there is a guide layer, the motion path is also scaled.

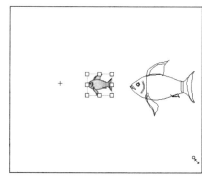

Naming an Instance

Once you create your movie clip symbol, you can drag an instance onto the stage and name it in the Instance palette.

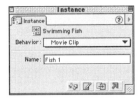

Creating Mask Layers

Mask layers enable you to hide or show portions of objects or animations that are linked to the mask layer. You can create both static and animated masks. If you have used Layer Masks in Photoshop, you will be familiar with the concept.

Simple Masks

A mask starts out as a simple image. You use solid colors to create it because the mask won't show gradients, fills, or Alphas. When the mask is working, it reveals only its shape. The layer you use for the mask must be *on top* of the layers that are to be masked.

1.

Create a new document and place an image into it or create an image.

2.

Create a new layer above the first one and draw or import the object you want to use for your mask. You may also use text as a mask.

3.

Ctrl+click (Mac) or right-click (Windows) the top layer between the symbols to show the Context menu. Select Mask.

You can also double-click the Layer Options icon at the left of the Layer list area and select Mask, but the masking process is a several-step affair when you do. You need to set the lower layer as a masked layer and then select Show Masking to see the effect of the mask. However, selecting Mask from the Context menu does everything with one mouse click.

Mask Layer Options

You can show or hide the mask, add layers to it, or remove the masking from the layer.

Hiding/Showing the Mask

You can toggle between showing and hiding the masking effect by Opt/Alt+clicking the name of the *masked* layer.

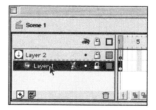

Editing a Mask or Masked Layer

You need to unlock the layers before you can make any changes to them. Unlocking the layers hides the masking feature. Lock the layers when you have finished to restore the masked effect.

Be sure to deselect all areas on the layers before you lock the layers again. If you have a selection in the Mask layer when you lock the layer, that selection might not show up as part of the mask.

Adding Masked Layers

You can add layers in several ways. If you make the lowest masked layer active and add a new layer above it, the new layer is automatically masked. You can also add a layer below the bottom masked layer. Double-click its layer name to open the Layer Properties dialog box. Select Masked as the layer type. If you don't see the full masked effect, choose Show Masking from the Context menu for each layer until the masking appears as it should.

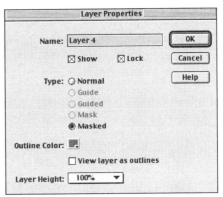

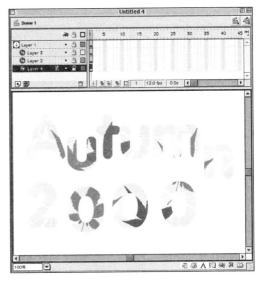

Unlinking Masked Layers

To remove a layer from participating in a mask effect, drag it above the mask layer. You can also change its layer type to Normal in the Layer Properties dialog box.

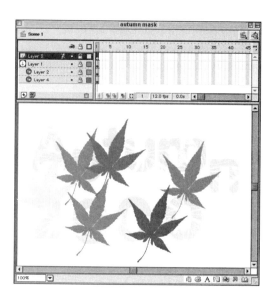

Masking Animations

A mask isn't really worth much if all it does is sit there masking a static image. You'll get more benefit out of the mask if you use it to mask an animation.

1.

Create a layer to animate. Add a motion tween, a shape tween, or whatever animation effect you want.

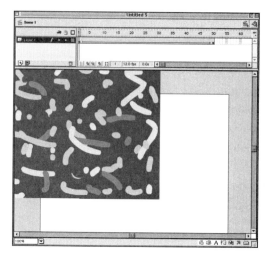

2.

Add a layer above it and create or import a static object for the mask.

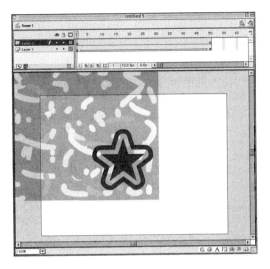

3.

Change the static object into a mask layer.

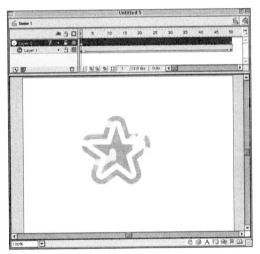

4.

Test and refine the animation. By changing the location of the much larger image in Layer 1, you can make it look as if a texture or image is moving through a single object (the mask).

Animating Masks

You can also create an interesting effect by animating the mask rather than the object being masked. Instead of creating the animation in the masked layer, create it in the mask layer before you change it into a mask. When you animate the mask instead of the masked layer from the Masking Animations section, it looks as if both the object and the texture move.

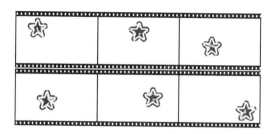

Three-Layer Animated Mask Effect

For example, if you animate a mask over two identically shaped but different-colored static background objects and only one of them is part of the mask, you can simulate light crossing an object.

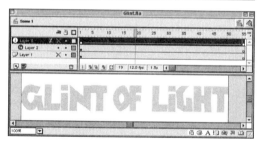

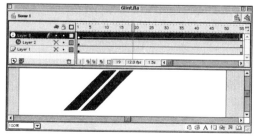

It's All in the Timing

You can change the timing of your animations after you've created them. Changing the timing can help you smooth out the action, reverse animations, or stretch or shrink the Timeline.

Stretching an Animation

To make an animation longer, drag its last keyframe toward the right in the Timeline. To make the animation shorter, drag the last keyframe toward the left. If the animation is a shape or motion tween, Flash automatically adjusts the tween. In a cel animation, move the keyframes manually to compensate. With multiple motion or shape tween keyframes on a layer, move the intermediate keyframes manually—Flash adjusts only the last tween.

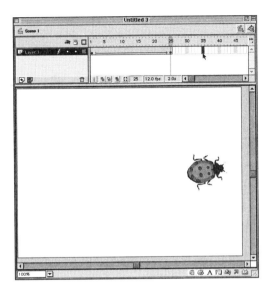

Removing Keyframes

To remove a keyframe, select the keyframe by clicking it in the Timeline. Choose Insert|Clear Keyframe (Shift+F6).

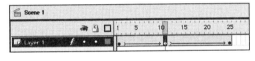

Smoothing the Action

Drag the keyframes anywhere in the Timeline to smooth out the animation. This feature is particularly useful with cel animation. You can add blank keyframes anywhere in the Timeline to hold the action for an additional frame or two.

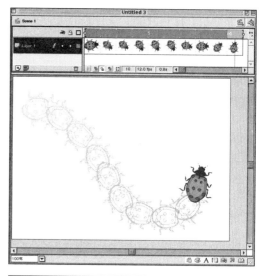

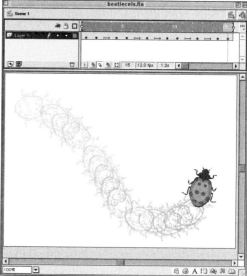

Reversing an Animation

You can copy frames and then paste and reverse them to make the animation play backward. With the Reverse command, you create the keyframes to animate half the layer and then create the other half to reverse the actions.

1.

Create an animation half as long as you want the final animation to be.

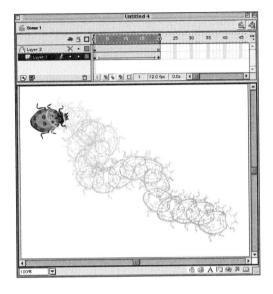

2.

Cmd/Ctrl+click the first frame to select it. Hold the Shift key and Cmd/Ctrl+click the last frame in the range to select the entire range.

This is a new behavior for selecting some of the frames on a layer. You can change this behavior by setting your preferences back to Flash 4 selection methods.

3.

Ctrl+click (Mac) or right-click (Windows) and choose Copy Frames from the Context menu.

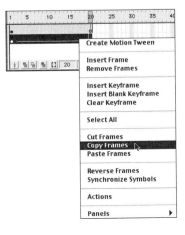

4.

Select the empty frame to the right of the last keyframe. Ctrl+click (Mac) or right-click (Windows) and choose Paste Frames from the Context menu.

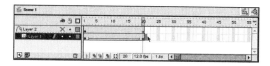

5.

Cmd/Ctrl+click the first pasted keyframe. Then hold the Shift key and Cmd/Ctrl+click the ending pasted keyframe to select the range of keyframes.

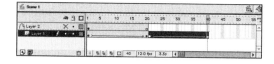

6.

Ctrl+click (Mac) or right-click (Windows) and choose Reverse Frames from the Context menu. Your animation now plays forward and backward.

Although Flash reverses the actions, it doesn't reverse the object being animated. If you want a motion-tweened ladybug to follow a motion path across the screen and then follow it back to its starting point, rotate the object being animated at the keyframe that begins the reversed animation and at the last keyframe on the reversed animation.

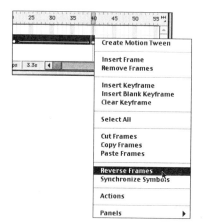

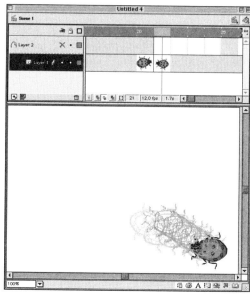

Moving an Entire Animation

To move an animation on the stage, unlock all the layers and choose Onion All. Turn on the Edit Multiple Frames feature. Choose Edit|Select All and drag the entire animation to a new location on the stage.

Only unlocked and visible layers can be moved. If you don't want to move a specific layer, lock or hide it before you move the animation. You can also select only a range of frames to move if you don't want to rearrange the entire movie.

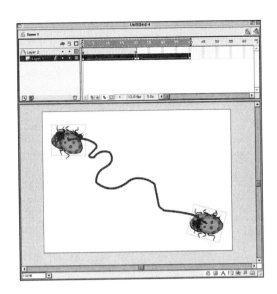

Making the Scene

Flash always adds a default Scene 1 to a movie. You can either create your entire movie in Scene 1 or add scenes. A movie, by default, plays continuously from the start to the end and jumps from scene to scene without pausing. However, scenes can help you organize a movie. If you create a Web site to feature three products, each product description can be in a different scene. You can also create a scene for the home page and for an order form page. You'll learn in Chapter 7 how to start and stop an action so that the scenes don't play straight through.

Adding a Scene

You can add a scene using two methods.

1.

To add a new scene, choose Insert|Scene.

2.

To add a new scene, you can also choose Window|Panels|Scene and click the Add Scene icon in the Scene panel.

Selecting a Scene to View

View a different scene by clicking the scene in the Scene panel or by choosing the desired scene in the Scene drop-down menu at the top-right of the Timeline window.

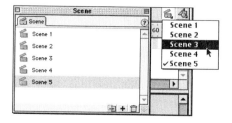

Renaming a Scene

Rename a scene by double-clicking on its name in the Scene panel and typing the new name.

Reordering a Scene

Reorder scenes by dragging the scene you want to move to a new location in the Scene panel.

Deleting a Scene

Delete a scene by selecting the scene in the Scene panel and click the Trashcan icon.

Duplicating a Scene

Duplicate a scene by clicking the Duplicate Scene icon in the Scene panel.

Previewing the Scene

To test only the current scene, choose Control|Test Scene.

Creating Frame Labels

You can label specific frames so that you can refer to them later. If you want to use any of Flash's ActionScripting or Frame Actions, you must label the frames.

1.

Insert a new layer at the top of the layer list to use only for the labels. You can insert a label on any layer, but creating a layer just for labels makes finding them much easier.

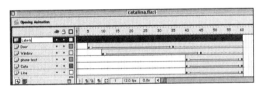

2.

Select the frame to label in the Label layer. In the Frame panel, type the name of the frame. The name appears in the Timeline at the specified frame.

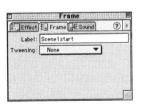

Because you are inserting labels in a layer that has no object, you must place a keyframe for every label that you want to enter. You can label only frames that contain keyframes. Select the frame on the labels layer and press F6 to create the keyframe. Then type the label.

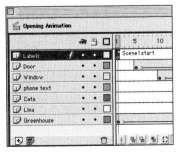

Loading and Unloading Movies

Flash lets you compile movies (.swf files) inside—or in place of—the main movie. You can create an endless loop of individual movies or load several movies to play at one time. You can even play several different movies at one time. If you string together individual movies, your project loads faster (because smaller files load faster than larger ones, and individual pieces will always load faster than the entire movie). Multiple movies can load on the same browser page, which eliminates the delay in invoking additional HTML pages. You can also replace a movie clip with an .swf version of the clip using the Load Movie command.

The Load Movie Command (into a Level)

The Load Movie command uses the Frame Actions panel. You'll meet more Frame and Object Actions in Chapters 7 and 8. In the example shown, individual movies load onto the page as banner ads. The background color of a movie drops out when the movie is loaded, which makes loaded movies transparent and means they can be placed on top of each other.

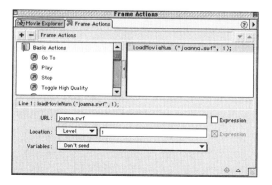

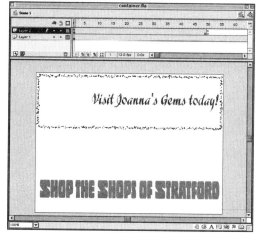

Movies and Levels

You load a movie into one of Flash's "imaginary" levels. Level 0 is the main Timeline—the Timeline of the movie that is the container. The movie loaded into Level 0 sets the frame rate, background color, and frame size of all other loaded movies. If you load a new movie into Level 0, you replace the main movie; loading a movie into any level that already has a movie replaces the original movie. You can load a movie into a level with a higher number and show it "on top of" the loaded movie. To load multiple movies at the same time, give them different level numbers. When you then use the Load Movie command, it places the new movie at the upper-left corner of the movie that loaded it.

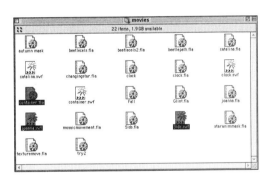

Joanna.fla Timeline

Loads into Level 1

Main Timeline: Level 0

Load Movie URLs

When you use the Load Movie command, you need to include either the absolute or a relative URL for the movie. While you are testing the movie, however, only the relative URL will work. Also, all the movies called from a main movie must be in the same physical folder on your hard drive. You might want to keep the movies in the same folder when you place them on the Web as well.

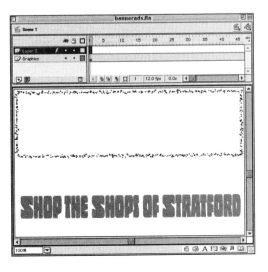

1.

Create a new layer to hold your actions and labels. Select the frame on the new layer from which to call the Load Action command.

To add the Frame Action to any frame other than the first frame in a layer, press F6 first to add a keyframe.

2.

Double-click the keyframe to open the Frame Actions panel. Click the Basic Actions button to see a list of actions that are suitable for a new user of Flash to try. They don't require much (if any) programming knowledge.

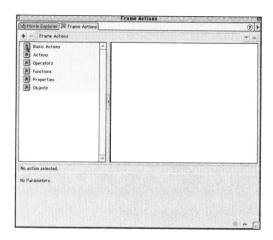

3.

Double-click the Load Movie command. Enter the desired level in the dialog box. In the URL field, type the unqualified name of the movie file to load (just the file name with no path). (Passing variables is beyond the scope of this book, and won't be needed in any exercise here.) As soon as you've entered the URL and level, the action is accepted.

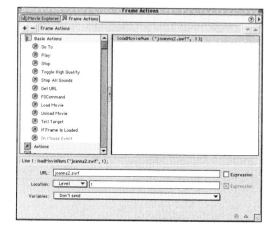

4.

The Timeline shows a tiny cursive letter *a* over the keyframe in the Actions layer.

Load Movie and Timelines

When you load a movie into another movie, the loaded movie uses its own Timeline, just as a movie clip does. However, if you are planning to replace the loaded movie with another movie (as in the banner ad example), you have two choices: you can leave room on your main movie Timeline for each movie that runs in that location, or you can set up each movie to call the next movie. Your first loaded movie, joanna.swf, could contain the Load Movie command to load sids.swf into Level 1; sids.swf would load joanna.swf again into Level 1 when it finished.

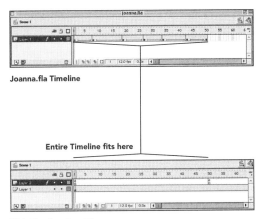

Joanna.fla Timeline

Entire Timeline fits here

Main Timeline: Level 0

The Load Movie Command (Replace Target)

Using the Load Movie command, you can also replace a movie clip with an .swf file. This technique lets you determine where to load the movie in the main movie window. The Load Movie Into Level command always uses the top-left corner of the calling movie, and there's no way to alter the location of the top-left corner. The Load Movie Into Target version of the command places the top-left corner of the loaded movie in the *center* of the movie clip (at the position of the crosshair registration point that's visible in editing mode).

1.

Create a movie clip to replace. Because the movie clip won't be seen, you might as well create a tiny rectangle as a movie clip symbol and use an Alpha of 0 to make it invisible. Position the invisible movie clip symbol into your image where you want the top-left corner of the loaded movie to appear.

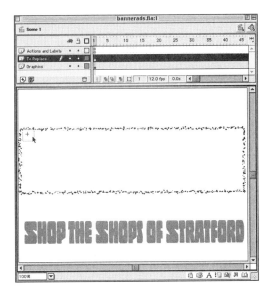

2.

After you position the instance of the movie clip, you need to name the instance in the Instance panel. You can't replace an unnamed instance.

3.

In the Actions And Labels layer, add a keyframe in which to call the Load Movie command. In the Frame Actions panel, change the Location drop-down to Target. Type the instance name into the Target field.

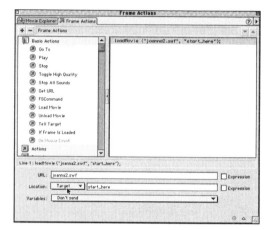

4.

The top-left of the movie now plays at the registration point of the replaced movie clip.

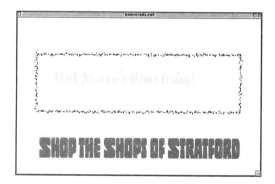

The Unload Movie Command

Use the Unload Movie command to remove a movie from memory. If you are loading a new movie into the same location, you don't need the Unload Movie command; a new movie at the same level replaces the previous one. However, if you load a movie into Level 1 and another one into Level 2 and don't want them both active, you must issue an Unload Movie command. You can unload a movie in either a Level or Target.

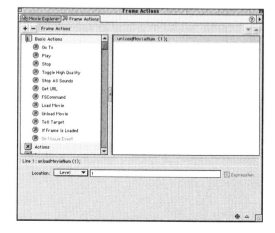

An Alternate Approach to Scenes

For a movie file to play, the entire file must download from the Web to the user's computer. Although the movie streams (that is, it plays as it downloads), downloading can still take a long time if you create a long movie or complex Web site (with or without using scenes). Many Flash professionals prefer to create the movie in scenes and replace each scene with an .swf version of the scene.

1.

Create your movie in scenes as you normally would.

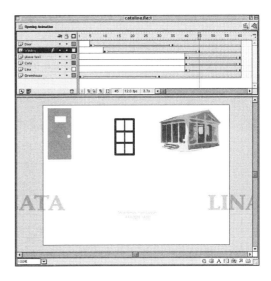

2.

When each scene is complete, save the file, then choose Control|Test Scene. The scene is rendered and saved to your hard drive with the default name pattern of filename_scenename. You can either change the name of the rendered scene or use that name as a reference.

3.

In your original movie, create a Labels And Actions layer and delete the other layers in the scene. Make sure that the Timeline is as long as it was originally. Insert a Load Movie command in the first keyframe on your only layer. When you are finished, the scene should contain nothing but the action itself.

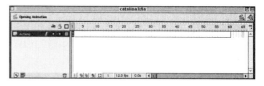

Chapter 6
Adding Sound

- Attach sound clips

- Edit sound

- Learn about event sounds and streaming sounds

- Synchronize sounds

- Learn about sound actions

- Export movies with sound

By Dan London

Sound Files and Compression

Audio files take up a massive amount of bandwidth. Because of this, Flash supports a number of compression schemes to decrease file size. Sounds that are used in Flash range from quick one-shot sounds, such as a beep, to complete songs. Flash supports both streaming and nonstreaming audio. Each has its advantages and disadvantages.

File Formats

Flash can import two types of noncompressed audio: WAV files (Windows only) and AIFF files (Macs only). Flash 5 can also import certain compressed audio types, the main one being MP3. If you have QuickTime 4 on your system, Flash can additionally import Sun AU files, Sound Designer II files (Macs only), Sound Only QuickTime Movie files, System 7 Sound files (Macs only), and WAV files for Macintosh.

Once the files have been imported, they will need to be compressed. Flash's compression schemes are as follows:

- *ADPCM*—This compression method is used for short sounds, such as a beep or car horn.
- *MP3*—Use this choice for all sounds that are more than one shots, such as music loops or voiceovers. This compression also works for simple sounds.
- *RAW*—This option allows you to export noncompressed audio from your Flash movies without degradation of the original audio. This setting should be used only locally or if users viewing and listening to your movies have a very fast connection (T1) and have computers equipped with powerful processors, or if the users will view your movie clip from a CD-ROM. For general Web use, you should avoid this setting.

Attaching Sound Clips

Attaching sounds to your movie is just like attaching a graphic or an animated symbol. It's as simple as dragging the sound clip from the Library onto the stage. The sound will occupy as many frames as it takes to play the sound in its entirety. If the sound clip has more frames than the movie does, the waveform will cut off visually at the last frame; however, depending on the settings you choose, it can continue to play even though the animation has finished. We will cover this option later in the chapter.

Keep in mind that a sound clip is measured in time, not in frames per second. Whether your movie plays at 10 frames per second or 20 frames per second does not affect the speed of the sound clip.

Simple Sounds

Let's begin with an example of attaching a sound to a button state.

1.

Open the Common Library (Window|Common Libraries|Buttons) and drag an instance of the Pill button onto the stage.

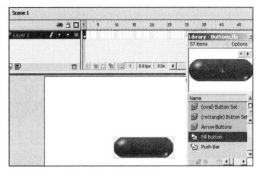

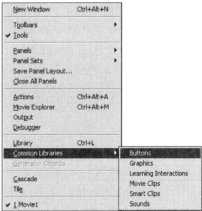

2.

Right-click the Pill button and choose Edit In Place. Add a new layer to the Timeline and name it Sounds.

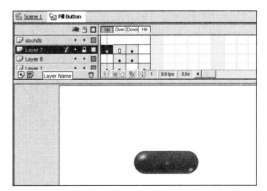

3.

Open the Window|Common Libraries|Sounds menu. Insert a keyframe on the Over state of the Sounds layer. From the Sounds Library, drag an instance of the Door Cls Click Rattle sound onto the stage. Notice how the waveform appears in the Timeline.

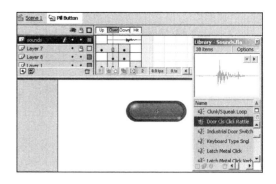

4.

Return to the main Timeline. Select Control|Enable Simple Buttons. Roll over the Pill button and listen to the effect.

Sound Loops

One way to cut down on file size is to use a music loop. The actual music may last for five seconds, but looping it makes it play continuously without adding to the download time.

1.

Create a new movie and name it soundloops.fla.

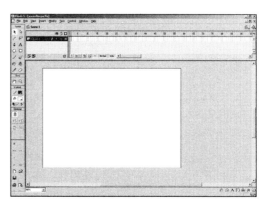

2.

Select and import the loopy.wav (Windows) or loopy.aif (Mac) file found on the *Flash 5 Visual Insight* ftp site (**ftp.coriolis.com** in the Public/ Flash5VI folder). This sound will now appear in the Library for this movie.

3.

Change the name of Layer 1 to Sounds. Open the Library (Ctrl/Cmd+L). Drag an instance of the loopy.wav sound clip onto the stage. Add a frame to Frame 45 to see the entire waveform.

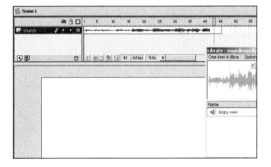

4.

Add a frame on Frame 300. Open the Sound panel. With the sound wave selected, type "4" in the Loops field. (Specifying that something loops once means it plays only once, so it's not really looping.)

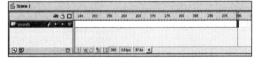

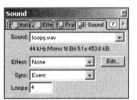

5.

Select Control|Test Movie and listen to the sound as it loops. Notice that it is a bit choppy. You will fix this in the next section.

Editing Sound

The best way to create a seamless loop is to use an audio editing program such as Sound Forge or Peak Bias. If all you need to do is tweak the volume or change a Start or Stop point, then Flash can do the trick. For more precise editing, you should investigate one of the other programs.

Setting Start and Stop Points

Start and Stop points can be used for a couple of different purposes: You can edit a loop or create different sounds from the same source.

1.

Return to soundloops.fla and select the sound wave in the Timeline. Open the Sound panel and choose Edit. The waveform should appear in the Edit Envelope pop-up window.

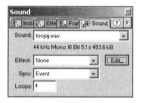

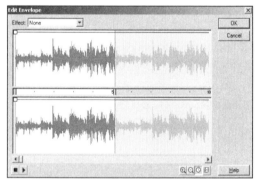

2.

Adjust the Start and Stop points by dragging the Time In and Time Out controls. Because the sound is looped, the looped part is grayed out. When you adjust a Start or Stop point, the position will appear in the looped section of the sound as well. Adjust the points until the loop sounds smooth.

Use the Zoom-In and Zoom-Out buttons to view the waveform as a whole or to zoom in on the audio. Zooming in lets you find breaks in the waveform and find the proper place to set the Start and Stop points. Find the place where the patterns change and try placing in and out points there.

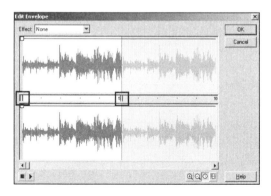

3.

Test the movie. Make sure the loops are seamless. If not, readjust the Start and Stop points for the sound clip.

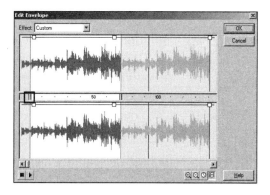

Setting Sound Envelopes

Sound envelopes are rough volume controls for the sound. When you adjust the way a sound fades in and out, you are adjusting the envelope. Flash comes with some premade effects, such as fading in and out or fading from left to right for a stereo sound.

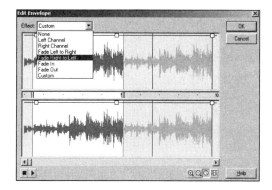

1.

Open the loopy.wav sound file in editing mode. Choose Fade Out from the Effects drop-down menu. Listen to the results.

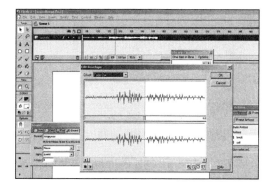

2.

Choose each effect and listen to how it changes the sound file. The grayed sections are the looped sections. You can create custom effects in each loop.

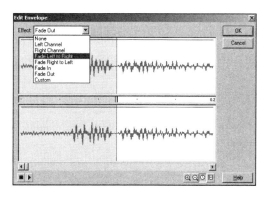

3.

To create an envelope handle, click the waveform. Click to the right of the first envelope
point and create a new point. Fade in the first
loop to that point by dragging the beginning
envelope point to the bottom of the waveform.

Remember that because this is a stereo sound,
you need to change the envelopes in the left
and right channels.

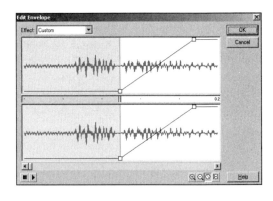

4.

At the end of the second loop, click the top of
the waveform and drag the envelope point
downward to create a custom fade out. Then
create a new envelope point to the right of the
fade so you can fade the loop back in.

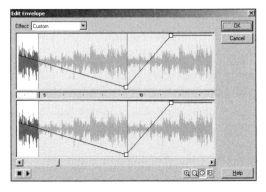

5.

Go to the fourth loop. Fade in the left channel
and fade out the right channel.

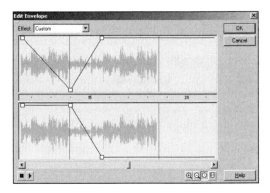

Event Sounds and Streaming Sounds

Flash syncs sounds in two different ways: by treating the sound as an *event* or by *streaming* the sound clip. The choices are available within the Sound panel from the Sync drop-down menu.

Event Sounds

An event sound is triggered by a keyframe and plays the sound in its entirety. If you choose Event from the Sync menu, the sound plays every time the event is triggered. For example, if the sound is attached to the Down state of a button, the sound plays each time the button is triggered.

Choosing Start as the Sync event causes the sound to play in its entirety before the sound can be played again. Choosing Stop as the Sync event stops the sound. Choosing Stop will allow you to start a sound at Frame 20 and stop it at Frame 40 even if the sound has not finished playing.

For simple sounds that are associated with button states or a single frame of animation, choosing event syncing is the way to go.

1.

Import a sound that is more than five seconds long and place it on the stage at Frame 20 of a layer.

2.

Click the waveform in the Timeline. Choose Start from the Sync drop-down menu in the Sound panel.

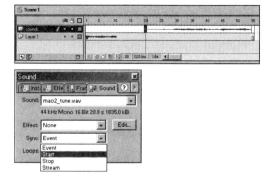

3.

Insert a keyframe (F6) at Frame 40. Drag another instance of the sound clip and choose Stop from the Sync drop-down menu.

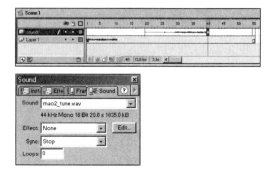

Streaming Sounds

The other type of syncing in Flash is streaming. Streaming forces the animation to keep up with the sound clip. The sound clip takes precedence over the movie, and frames of animation are dropped if necessary to keep the sound playing. For a voiceover or a cartoon where the sound needs to sync with certain sections of animation, you should choose streaming.

Synchronizing Sounds

Like graphics, sound clips can be made into movie clips. The advantages are that the sound clip will not be affected by the main Timeline and that the clip can be loaded and unloaded as needed, which can cut down on file size. Basically, using audio movie clips creates the same advantages as using graphic movie clips. To turn a sound clip into a movie clip, follow these steps:

1.

Select Insert|New Symbol or Cmd/Ctrl+F8. Choose Movie Clip as its behavior and name the clip accordingly.

2.

Within the movie clip Timeline, drag an instance of the sound clip onto the stage.

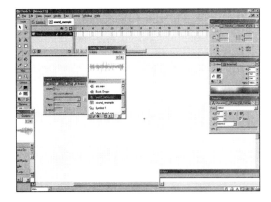

3.

Insert a frame at about Frame 500 and either remove or add frames until you reach the end of the waveform.

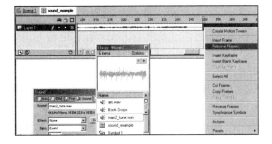

Sound Actions

Sometimes you want to let users choose whether to hear sound while viewing your Flash movie. Some viewers might not have sound capabilities on their systems, and forcing them to stream audio slows down the performance for no reason. The way around this is adding a Stop All Sounds action, usually associated with a button.

1.

Open a Flash movie that contains sound clips. Create a button and place it on the stage.

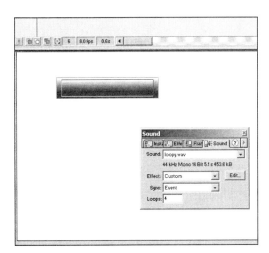

2.

Right-click the button to open the Object Actions panel. Click the + in the upper-left corner and choose Stop All Sounds from the Actions drop-down menu.

When the user clicks and releases the button, all sound clips will turn off.

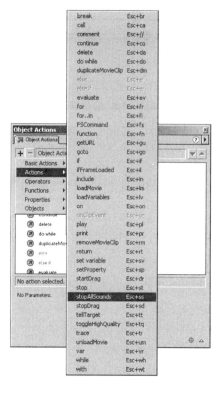

3.

If you want the user to be able to turn off only certain sounds, such as loops, but not the individual simple sounds along the Timeline, place the loops and the Stop All Sounds button within a movie clip. The Stop All Sounds action affects only the sounds within that movie clip.

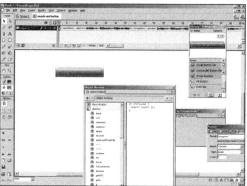

Exporting Movies with Sound

Your final task before finishing your sound clips is to choose the compression settings. Flash comes with default settings for all your sounds in the same way it does for images. But there will be times when you can cut the quality of one sound clip to allow a more important clip within your movie to be of higher quality.

There are two ways to choose compression settings for your sound clips: using the Publish Settings window, or compressing sound clips individually.

1.

Open a movie and choose File|Publish Settings.

2.

Click the Flash tab. Click the Set button for the Audio Stream or Audio Event and choose your compression settings from the drop-down menu.

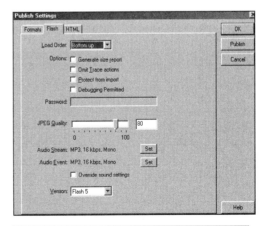

3.

The second way of compressing audio is to compress your sound clips individually from within the Library. Open a Library with sound clips inside it and either double-click the clip or right-click it and choose Properties. Choose your compression settings from the drop-down menu in the Sound Properties panel.

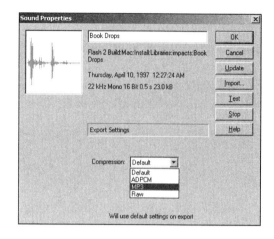

4.

Within this window, not only can you change the settings for each file, but you can also hear a preview of the compressed sound by clicking the Test button.

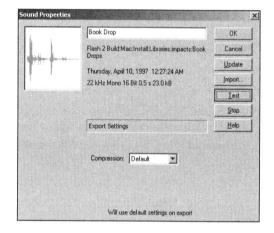

5.

If you choose a compression setting other than the default, the file size and the amount of compression compared to the original will appear in the window. Also from this window, you can update the sound if you edited it outside Flash. You can also change the file name or import a new sound into your Library.

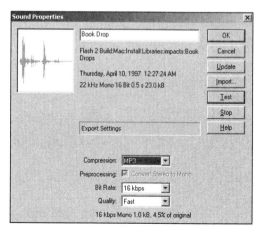

Sound Settings

Within the Settings menu, you have a choice of Disabled, ADPCM, MP3, or RAW.

- *ADPCM*—Gives a sound quality of 5kHz to 44.1kHz and a 2 to 5Kbps bit rate. Converting stereo sounds to mono is a sure way to decrease file size, and most users won't notice a difference. Because the ADPCM setting is used for short sounds, using higher-quality settings probably won't add much to your file size. However, because they are short sounds, lower quality might not affect them much either. The best thing to do is experiment while checking the Bandwidth Profiler, which will be covered in Chapter 9.

- *MP3*—Gives you the choice of speed settings from 8Kbps to 160Kbps and quality settings of Fast, Medium, or Best. The default is 16Kbps and Fast. Because MP3 streaming is used for long sounds, music loops, and voiceovers, this setting is very important. MP3s are the best way to compress audio for the Web, and they can deliver near CD-quality audio in a drastically reduced file size. Saying that, the file size difference between audio at 16Kbps and 160Kbps is huge. Always try for the lowest-quality audio that doesn't degrade your audio to unrecognizable mush. MP3 compression can do strange things to your audio, so experimenting with settings is key.

- *RAW*—Gives you the choice of 5kHz to 44.1kHz settings. If you import CD-quality audio and want to export it at the same rate, choose 44.1kHz. Remember, though, that this setting will make your movie undeliverable on the Web for all but the fastest connection speeds.

Chapter 7
Buttons and Interactivity

- Learn to create button symbols

- Learn to create rollovers and disjoint rollovers

- Learn to set button events

- Use the Tell Target command

- Learn to construct menus

By Sherry London

The Button Symbol

Buttons are symbols that let you add interactivity to your animations. A user clicks a button to trigger an action—going to a new Web page, showing more information, or playing a sound or another animation. Flash has a special symbol, called the button symbol, for this special type of interaction. A button symbol contains its own four-frame Timeline. Each frame on the Timeline is called a *state*. The states are: Up (nothing is pressed or selected), Over (the mouse moves the cursor on top of the button symbol), Down (the mouse button is pressed), and Hit (a state that defines the real estate occupied by the button).

Creating a Button Symbol

Buttons can be as simple as a circle or as complex as an embedded movie clip. To create a button, the minimum you need is a shape.

1.

Create a shape or shapes and choose Insert|Convert To Symbol. Choose Button as the symbol type.

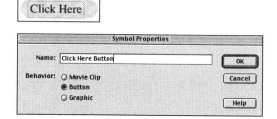

2.

Double-click the Button symbol to enter Symbol Edit mode. The Timeline for the button symbol consists of four frames: Up, Over, Down, and Hit. Only the Up state contains a keyframe. The symbol as it appears in this keyframe is the version of the button that the user sees when the page launches.

3.

Select the Over state and add a keyframe (F6). Modify the symbol so that it looks different when a mouse rolls over it by changing the color, size, orientation, or any other facet of the button as you wish. If you use an embossed button, you can make the button look pressed rather than "up." You can embed a movie clip symbol in this state to create an animated rollover.

4.

Select the Down state and add a keyframe (F6). This state shows the button in the split second when the mouse button is clicked. You can change the symbol as you please. However, if you want something to occur when the user clicks the button, you need to attach an action to it. Sometimes, you don't want this state to be active. You are not required to define a Down state on a button.

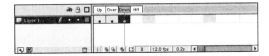

5.

To create the Hit state, place a keyframe in the Hit state on the Timeline. The Hit state is invisible to the user. It identifies to Flash the screen area that is the button. The Hit state does not need to be the same shape as the button—it can be larger, but should never be smaller. You can fill the button shape with black for the Hit state.

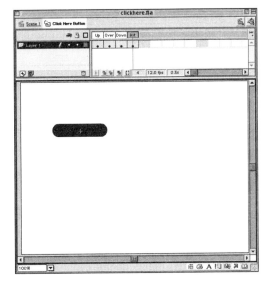

Testing a Button

If you enable buttons, you can preview the buttons in Flash. You can also compile the animation and test it in the Flash Player.

Enabling Simple Buttons

To let button states appear in the Flash editor, choose Control|Enable Simple Buttons. When the buttons are enabled, you can't move or select them with the Arrow tool, so you'll need to toggle the Enable Simple Buttons off and on as you work.

Control	
Play	Return
Rewind	⌥⌘R
Step Forward	.
Step Backward	,
Test Movie	⌘Enter
Debug Movie	⇧⌘Enter
Test Scene	⌥⌘Enter
Loop Playback	
Play All Scenes	
Enable Simple Frame Actions	
Enable Simple Buttons	⌥⌘B
Mute Sounds	

You can still select buttons using the Arrow tool.

Creating Rollovers

A *rollover* is an action that occurs when the user's mouse is on top of a button Hit state and Flash shows the associated Over frame in the button Timeline. The Over frame can hold an image or an entire animation. Depending on the relationship between the location of the Hit state and the button's Over state, the action can look as if it is happening to the original button or to something else on the screen.

Simple Rollovers

To create a simple rollover in which the image in the Over state changes, you need to modify the Up state image. The most common modification is to create a version of the button that looks as if someone has physically pressed the button down. However, the possibilities are limitless. You can create a totally different image if you want.

Disjoint Rollovers

A *disjoint* or *remote* rollover occurs when you roll over a button, and something else on the screen changes. The main tricks to creating disjoint rollovers are deciding which item to make into the button and choosing where to place the Hit state.

1.

In the example shown, the text that appears inside the book is actually the button symbol. An Alpha effect applied to the Up state makes the text invisible.

2.

The Over state shows the text at 100 percent opacity.

3.

The Hit state is on top of an elf symbol. When a cursor rolls over that Hit state, the text appears.

An alternate way to construct the rollover is to define the elf as the button and leave the Hit state on the elf but add the text to the Over state.

Animated Rollovers

You can create animated rollovers by placing a movie clip in the Over state frame. In the example shown, you can create the Up state (nonanimated) by changing the Instance type to a single-frame graphic.

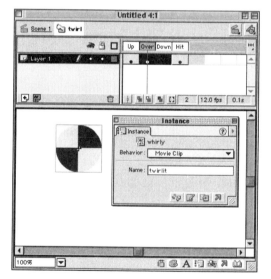

Creating Animated Buttons

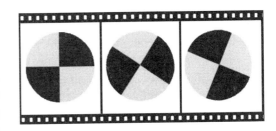

To animate the Up, Over, or Down state of a button symbol, replace the state with a movie clip symbol. Be cautious, however: Part of the animation should remain stationary so that it can be clicked. Although it is possible to create buttons that the user must catch to select, most users become annoyed when they need to play a game to select an option. You must use the Test Movie command to preview a button that contains an animation because you can't run movie clips in the editing environment.

Attaching Simple Sounds

You can attach a sound to the Up, Over, or Down state of a button. You can use the same sound in each state, choose a different sound, or edit the sound so that it seems different for each state.

1.

Select the button symbol in the Library panel.

2.

Double-click the button symbol you want or choose Edit from the Library Options menu to enter edit mode. Add a layer for sound in the Button Timeline.

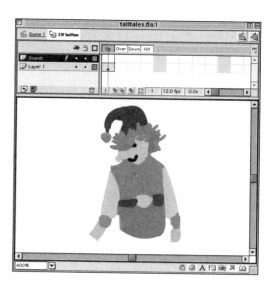

3.

In the sound layer, add a keyframe to the button state in which you want to add sound. To add a sound that plays when a mouse rolls over the button, place a keyframe in the Over state.

4.

With the playhead on the keyframe you have just created, drag the sound from either the Movie Library or the Sound Library into the Button editing window. The sound symbol is invisible in the window, but it appears in the sound layer at the playhead. If you have multiple sounds, pick the one you want from the Sound pop-up.

5.

Choose Event from the Sync pop-up menu in the Sound panel.

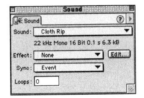

Introducing Button Actions

When played in a browser, Flash movies loop continuously and play from start to finish with no stops. To change this default behavior, you use actions with Stop or Play commands attached to them. Because one of the major purposes of using a button is to start, stop, or go to a particular part of a movie, you need to be able to attach actions to particular button states.

Go To (and Play)

One of the most common button actions is to tell Flash to go to another part of the Timeline and play the animation from there. You must perform several steps to make the command work properly.

1.

In the frame that contains the button, place a Stop action so that the animation waits until a button is selected.

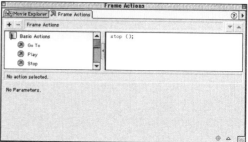

2.

Create the keyframe that will play when the button is clicked or create a new scene for the keyframe. Give the keyframe a unique label.

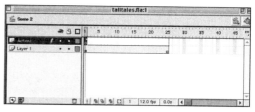

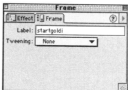

3.

Select the button to which you want to attach the action.

4.

If the Frames panel is not already open, click the Edit Actions icon at the bottom of the Instance panel.

5.

Double-click the Basic Actions icon to view the list of actions.

6.

Double-clicking the Go To action opens the dialog area below. The command is displayed in the panel to the right. The default mouse event is On Release, which makes the command execute if the user releases the mouse cursor in the Hit state area. The Go To command defaults to Go To And Play.

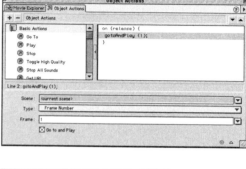

7.

Select the correct scene from the scene pop-up on the Object Actions panel.

8.

Select the desired method of specifying the Go To location from the Type pop-up. Choose Frame Label to advance to a specific labeled frame.

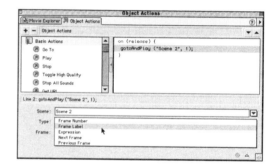

9.

Based on the Type you selected, choose the specific location in the Frame pop-up. If you selected Frame Label for the Type, the pop-up contains a list of labels in the movie.

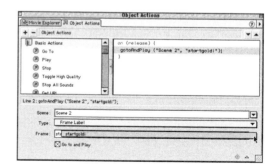

Button Events

Go To And Play or Go To And Stop are the most common button actions that a beginning Flash user chooses. Every action you apply to a button, however, must have a trigger—some specific mouse action in relation to that button that causes the button action to occur. You may attach more than one button event to a specific action. The default button event is On Release. The other button events are listed below.

On Press

The action occurs when the user presses the mouse button inside the Hit state area.

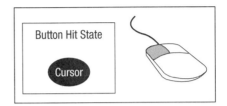

On Release Outside

The action occurs when the user presses the mouse button inside the Hit state area and releases the mouse button outside the Hit state area.

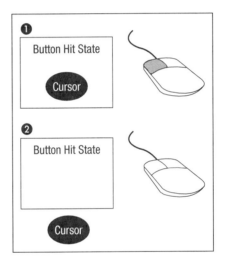

On Roll Over

A rollover occurs when the mouse cursor enters the Hit state area but the mouse button is not pressed.

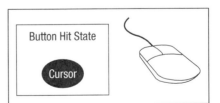

On Roll Out

The On Roll Out event occurs when the user rolls over the Hit state area and moves the cursor out of the Hit state area while not pressing the mouse button.

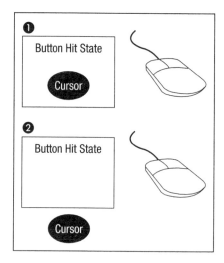

On Drag Over

The On Drag Over event occurs when the user presses the mouse button outside the Hit state area and keeps it pressed while moving the cursor into the Hit state area. This behavior is common when navigating a menu list.

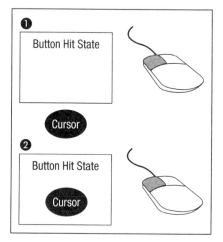

On Drag Out

The On Drag Out event occurs when the user keeps the mouse button pressed while leaving the Hit state area after first dragging over the Hit state area with the mouse button pressed. This behavior is common when navigating a menu list.

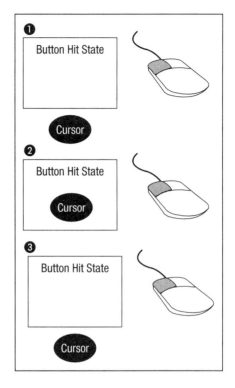

On Key Press

The On Key Press event lets you designate a specific keystroke to activate a button. Check the event checkbox and enter the letter to associate with the button.

Tell Target Command

You can attach actions to frames or objects. If you use movie clips or loaded movies, however, you need to be able to refer to their Timelines in an action. For example, you might want a button that tells a movie clip to start or stop playing. A movie clip uses its own Timeline—not the Timeline of the main movie. Therefore, you need to tell Flash to stop the movie clip's Timeline. The Tell Target command lets you refer to embedded Timelines.

Tell Target Setup

In the example shown here, the Propeller layer is a movie clip that rotates. The main movie animates this clip on a guide path that hugs the larger circle. The buttons start or stop the propeller from spinning as it circles around the guide path. To prepare the buttons for the Tell Target command, name the movie clip instance.

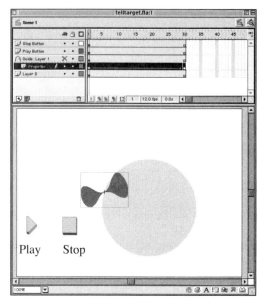

To create a circular guide path, leave a tiny gap in the path. If you don't, Flash takes the shortest distance between your starting and ending points, and the object won't move around the path.

Referencing Timelines

The Tell Target command works by letting you select the Timeline to reference.

1.

Select the button that will reference a movie clip's Timeline.

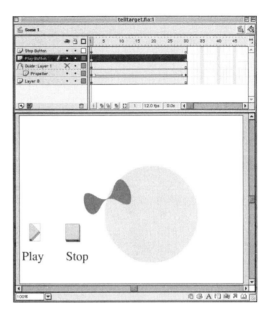

2.

Open the Object Actions panel and choose Tell Target from the Basic Actions group.

3.

Double-click the Tell Target command to transfer it to the right-hand panel.

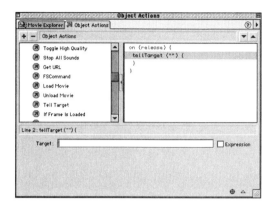

4.

Click the Insert A Target Path icon at the bottom right of the Object Actions panel.

If the Insert A Target Path icon is not active, double-click the Tell Target line in the right-hand section of the Object Actions panel.

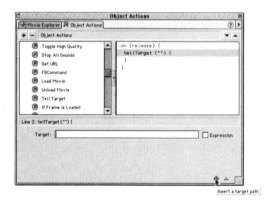

5.

Select the movie clip instance from the Insert Target Path dialog box by highlighting it. Click Dots Notation (Slashes Notation is accepted—but not suggested—in Flash 5). Relative Mode is safest as it displays only the named movie clip instances currently onstage (Flash can target only those instances that are onstage when the button is pressed). Absolute Mode displays all named movie clip instances and all loaded movies.

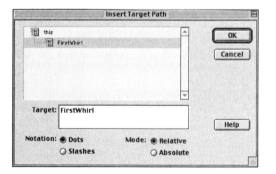

6.

The named instance is transferred into the command line. You may change the On Release to On Rollover or any other button event you prefer.

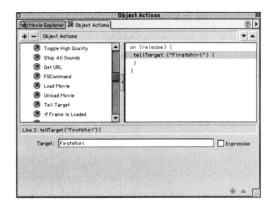

Making a Menu

Flash is frequently used to create menus on a Web site. Menus are more complex to create than simple buttons. To create interactive navigation systems, you use a combination of button actions and button Hit states. You can create menus that pop up options when you roll over or click the main buttons. You need to program the buttons to go to specific frames on your Timeline when they are selected. You also need to create logic to close the menu when a user rolls off the buttons. You can set buttons to behave like normal menu items that a user can drag through with the mouse button pressed.

Flash does not help you create the menus. You must construct all the logic to make the menu work. That logic can get complicated very quickly. In particular, the logic needed to make the buttons close so that the menus close properly in every possible situation can be very difficult to write. Because this is a beginner's book, here you'll learn two menu techniques that work in simple instances (and practice another simple variation in Chapter 13). To create a large number of nested menus, you will need more advanced programming than we cover here. However, the following techniques will get you started.

Creating Clickable Menus

Creating a menu that opens and closes only when you click on a button is easier than creating a menu that opens on a rollover.

Design a Main Menu Button Symbol

In a new movie, press Cmd/Ctrl+F8 to create a new button symbol. Name it MainMenu Button. Create Up, Over, and Down states. Unless you are making a circular or odd-shaped button, you don't need to create a specific Hit state.

Design a Submenu Button Symbol

Create another new button symbol (Insert|New Symbol or Cmd/Ctrl+F8). Name it Submenu Item. This button contains a rectangular Hit state to make it easier for the user to click.

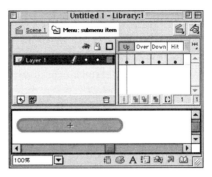

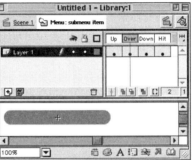

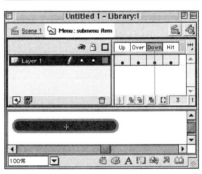

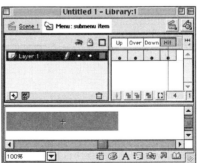

Create the Main Menu Graphic

In the main movie Timeline, create a background for your main menu. Place the main menu buttons on top of the background and add text labels for each button.

By adding text labels that are not part of the buttons, you can reuse your button symbol for each of the main menu options.

Add the Labels and Actions Layers

Create a new layer at the top of the layer list for Frame Actions and Frame Labels.

1.

Create a new layer named Frame Actions.

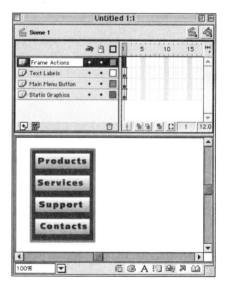

2.

Select Frame 1 on the Frame Actions layer and double-click Stop in the Basic Actions in the Frame Actions panel. Stop halts the playhead when the movie runs. Nothing else is executed until a button action specifically changes the location of the playhead.

You don't need to create a keyframe in Frame 1 on this layer—Flash automatically creates an unmarked keyframe when the layer is created. Without a keyframe, you couldn't select the frame and add an action or a label.

3.

Create a new layer named Frame Labels.

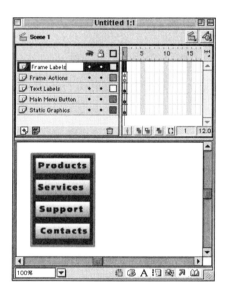

4.

Select Frame 1 in the Frame Labels layer. In the Frame panel, enter "Start" as the label for this frame.

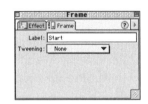

Why should you use Frame Labels? Frame Labels make it easier to move frames. If you drag the keyframes on Frame 10 to Frame 15, the labels travel with the keyframes and the actions still work. If you use only the frame number and move the keyframe, actions at that frame will no longer work—you have to locate all the places that call Frame 10 and change the reference, which is a major waste of time.

Create the Submenu Graphic

To create the button graphics for the submenus, first insert a keyframe for the first button and then build the submenu to display.

1.

Select Frame 10 on all five layers (press Shift+click to select multiple frames at once). Press F6 to insert keyframes in this location on every layer.

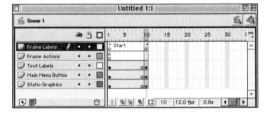

You don't need to use Frame 10 for the next keyframe—any empty frame will do. However, Frame 10 is easy to see and using it gives you enough room to see the Start label on the first layer of the Timeline.

2.

Select Frame 10 on the Frame Labels layer. In the Frame panel, enter an identifier for your first button label as the Frame Label.

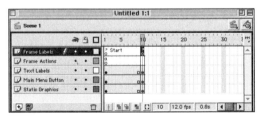

You can label the frame with any name you want, but it's easier to remember what the keyframes do if you give the labels meaningful names. You won't see the label name on the Timeline until you create more frames.

3.

Select the Main Menu Button layer and add a new layer named Submenu Buttons. This layer is for the submenu graphics.

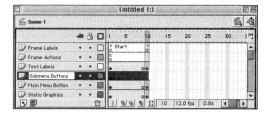

4.

With the playhead at Frame 10 and the Submenu Buttons layer active, create a keyframe (F6). Drag an instance of the Submenu Button symbol onto the stage.

If you don't insert a keyframe on a layer before you place an object on that layer, the object is assumed to begin in Frame 1. Because you want the button to be visible only at Frame 10, you must explicitly place a keyframe in Frame 10 on that layer.

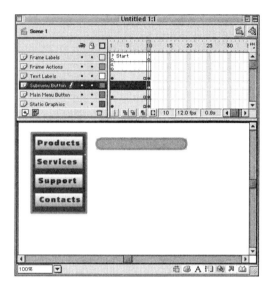

5.

Duplicate and arrange the submenu button instances. Create a layer for the submenu button text and create a text label for each button. (Be sure to add a keyframe at Frame 10 before you create your text labels, or the text objects are assumed to begin in Frame 1.)

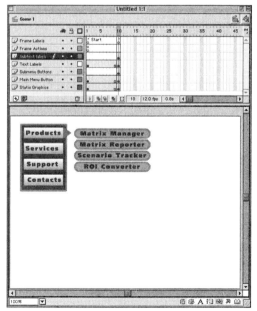

Duplicate the Submenu Graphics

You need to create a new frame location for every main menu button and move the submenu buttons into the correct spot for each of the sets of keyframes.

1.

Select Frame 20 in every layer and add a keyframe to the layers (F6).

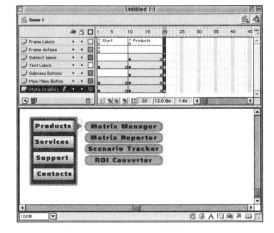

2.

Select Frame 20 in the Frame Labels layer and name the frame to correspond to the button that points to this frame.

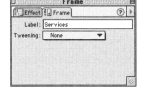

3.

With the Arrow tool, marquee-select the submenu buttons and any static graphics and labels that go with them. Don't select the main menu buttons. Drag the collection to the new location next to the second button in your main menu.

Use Shift+down arrow to move the selected objects quickly into the general position and then adjust their location with the down or up arrow key. Using the arrow keys ensures that your buttons line up from keyframe to keyframe.

4.

Repeat Steps 1 through 3 for each main menu button. If you have four buttons, you'll have four keyframe sets beyond the original Start label.

Create the Basic Menu Logic

Your menu won't work unless you add Button Actions. Each main menu button in *every* keyframe needs to contain an action that tells it what to do when clicked. The basic logic for this menu is that clicking a button opens its submenu. Clicking the same button closes the submenu. Clicking a different main menu button opens that button's submenu items and closes the open ones.

1.

Move the playhead to Frame 1 and select the first main menu button. In the Object Actions panel, double-click the Go To command in the Basic Actions section. Deselect the Go To And Play checkbox at the bottom of the panel. The command changes to Go To And Stop. Accept the default Release as the Button Event. Set the Type to Frame Label and the Frame to the label for that button (the Products button sends the playhead to the Products label). Repeat the process for each button visible in Frame 1.

Remember to click the button, not its text. You can't add an action to a text object. Also remember to deselect the Go To And Play checkbox in each button action (you need to stop the movie on each keyframe).

2.

Move the playhead to Frame 10 (or the keyframes called by the first main menu button if you didn't choose Frame 10). Select the first main menu button. If this button is clicked again, you want to send the playhead back to the Start label—the only frame on which none of the submenus are open. Sending the playhead back to Start closes all the menus. Again, you want a Go To And Stop action.

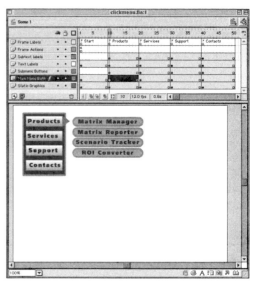

3.

The other main menu buttons on Frame 10 need to take the playhead to the same labels that they did on Frame 1. Only the button whose submenu is displayed on that frame needs to contain special logic. For each remaining button on Frame 10, enter the same Go To And Stop action as you did on Frame 1. Move the playhead to each of the remaining keyframes and repeat the process—send the button whose submenu is displayed back to Frame 1 and the rest of the buttons to their respective labels.

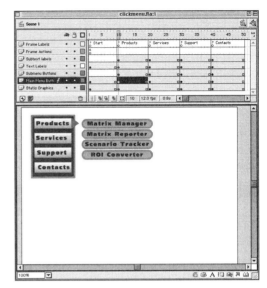

4.

Test the movie (Cmd+Return/Ctrl+Enter) to make sure that the main menu actions are properly defined. You need to test every button *from* every button. One common mistake is to leave the action set to Go To And Play instead of Go To And Stop.

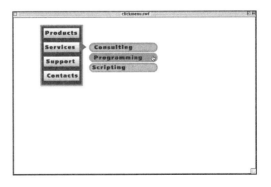

Create the Submenu Logic

Before you program the submenu buttons, you have a number of design decisions to make. What do you want to happen when the user clicks a specific submenu button? Do you need to clear the stage and make it look as if the user is choosing another HTML page? Do you want to call another HTML page (and movie), jump to new keyframes on the main Timeline or use scenes, load a new movie into the current one, or open a new window? You need to know the answers before you begin to implement your navigation system. If you decide to use scenes, create them before implementing the menus to make your testing process easier. Once you know where to send the user when a button is clicked, add the Go To action as you did for the main menu.

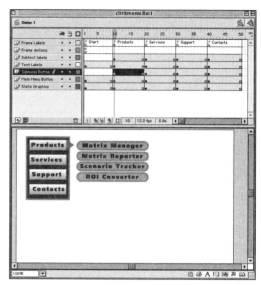

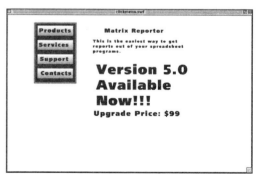

Track as Button

So far, you've been shown how to define only standard buttons. When a symbol is defined as a button, the Instance panel contains two options: Track As Button (the default) or Track As Menu Item. The default condition executes the rollover state of the button only when the mouse button is *not* pressed. On a menu, however, users frequently keep the mouse button pressed throughout the entire navigation process—especially on the Macintosh, which did not have "sticky" menus until System 8.0. Once you've chosen Track As Menu Item, the Down state is shown on rollover because the mouse button was pressed on a different button and not yet released. (That's why it's important to set your Actions to On Release rather than On Press.)

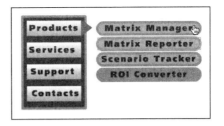

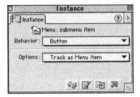

Creating an Invisible Hit State

If the user decides not to select any menu option, your menu should close. However, Flash doesn't provide a way to sense the user's mouse location automatically, so you need to create the logic yourself. The most common method is to position buttons around the menu and set them to go to the Start frame when they are rolled over. This technique assumes that an uninterested user will roll the mouse away from the buttons. You need these buttons to be invisible. The easiest way to create an invisible button is to create a button that has only a Hit state.

You'll learn another use for an invisible Hit state button in Chapter 13.

1.

Create a new layer at the very bottom of the layer list named Invisibles. You'll use this layer to place buttons that have only a Hit state (which is not visible).

2.

Insert a new button symbol. Name the symbol Invisible. Drag the keyframe from the Up state to the Hit state in the symbol's Timeline. Create a rectangle to indicate your Hit state. You can size each button instance, so you don't need to worry about the button size.

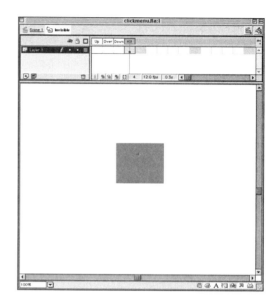

3.

In the main movie, drag the playhead to the frame that contains the last set of buttons (or the buttons that are the lowest on the screen). Drag an invisible button below the area that contains the submenu buttons and size it to fit the width of the window. The size will work even if the movie is viewed on a larger monitor. Make the button tall enough that a mouse will be "read" as it passes over.

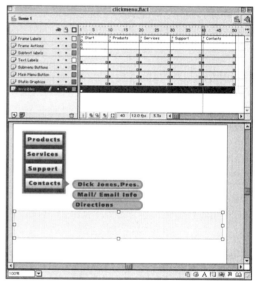

4.

Add a Go To And Stop action to the button. Change the Button Event to On Roll Over by checking Roll Over and unchecking the Release box.

5.

Drag copies of the button instance (with the action attached) to surround the menu and its submenus. Make sure that the invisible buttons touch.

Because each invisible button does the same thing, it doesn't matter which button is triggered. It also doesn't matter if invisible buttons are under the main menu; the button on top is always the active button. Just be sure that an invisible button isn't between the main menu and the submenu buttons, or your buttons won't work properly.

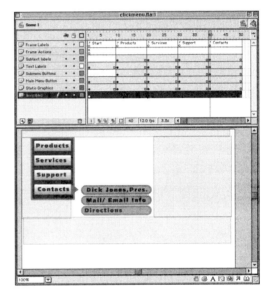

Create a Rollover Menu System

Flash 5 ships with an example called Track As Menu.fla, available through Help|Samples. This menu works much like the clickable menu discussed above. However, the submenus pop up when a mouse rolls over the associated buttons. Each button+submenu combination is stored as a movie clip.

The only problem with this system is that if you stack buttons, the menus don't always close properly. Because invisible buttons are embedded in the movie clip, they get in the way of other buttons that also have invisible Hit states. You should be able to understand the logic of this sample if you pull it apart. Just exercise some care when you use it and try not to have your menu options close to one another (which is difficult on a menu).

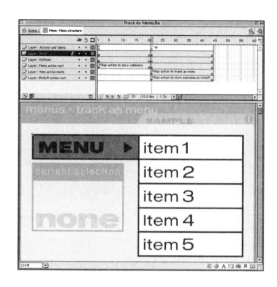

Dragging Movies

You can create interactivity in a movie by letting your user drag movie clips from one location on the stage to another. Macromedia uses this technique in its Flash training course to show how to construct a shopping basket, letting the user drop items into it that add to their invoice total. You could have users drag movie clips to create funny faces or create their own interface, or you could construct movable scroll bars. Flash lets you drag only one movie clip at a time. You attach a Start Drag action to a movie clip to start dragging it and a Stop Drag action to end the drag.

The Flash documentation claims you can drag only a button inside a movie clip. However, you can also use any movie clip and set On Clip Event to On Press.

Dragging a Button in a Movie Clip

To make a button draggable, you need to embed it in a movie clip.

1.

Insert a new button symbol into a movie. Create a button. You can create a button that contains only an Up state for this technique (although you may create a full-state button if you choose).

2.

Insert a new movie clip symbol into a movie.

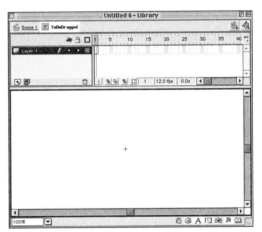

3.

Drag an instance of the button symbol from the movie Library into the movie clip. (You are in Edit mode when you first create a new symbol.)

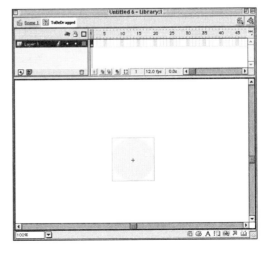

4.

While still in Edit mode, select the button. Double-click the startDrag Action in the Actions section of the Object Actions panel. Although the command has parameters, use the command as it is entered into the right pane of the panel.

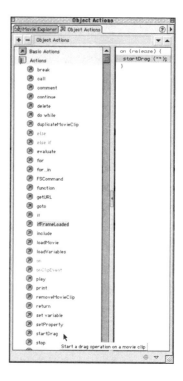

5.

Click the On Release line and select Press as the event instead. Deselect the Release checkbox.

6.

Click the last line of the Action to highlight it. Then double-click the stopDrag action.

To enter multiple commands for one object, select the last line of the previous command.

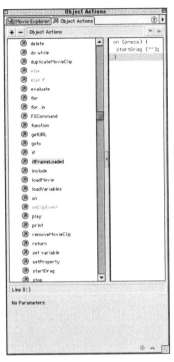

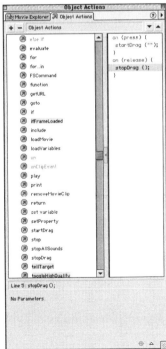

7.

Drag an instance of the movie clip into your main movie and test the movie. You should be able to easily drag and let go of the button.

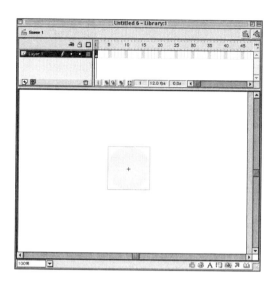

Dragging a Movie Clip

To create a draggable movie clip that doesn't contain a button, the procedure is almost the same.

1.

Create a new movie clip symbol.

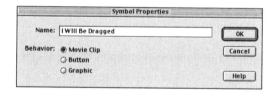

2.

Draw your symbol.

3.

Drag an instance of the symbol into the main movie Timeline and name the instance.

4.

Select the movie clip. Double-click the startDrag Action to add it to the object. Highlight the onClipEvent line and change the clip event to Mouse Down.

5.

Highlight the startDrag line again and select the Expression checkbox. Enter the instance name (with no quotes) as the expression.

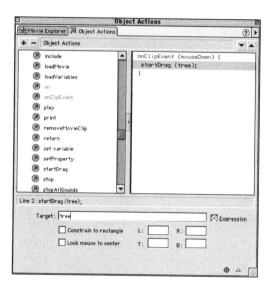

6.

Highlight the last command line and double-click the stopDrag action. Highlight the onClipEvent line and change the event to Mouse Up. No other changes are needed. Test your movie.

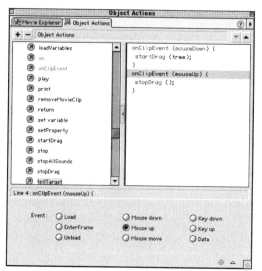

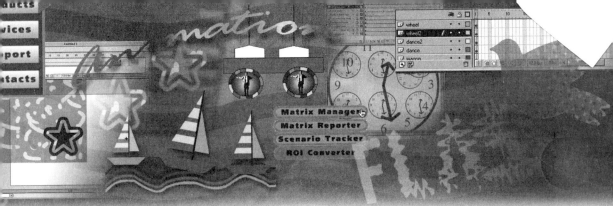

Chapter 8
Creating Interactive Forms

- Create editable text

- Use form validation

- Create check boxes

- Use Flash to do arithmetic

- Use smart clips

By Jennifer Hall

Creating Editable Text Boxes

Flash allows text to be displayed on screen and also allows the user to change the information using the text box on a Web page. Flash's text-handling features are very useful—for example, you can display a changing score or the name of the current user.

Specifying Editability

Flash gives you three editability options when you create a piece of text: static, dynamic, or input. Static text will not change. Dynamic text will be updated continuously, as in a constantly updated weather report. Input text is for user-changeable information or for displaying information that can be updated but seldom is.

1.

To choose the editability of text, begin by selecting the Text tool.

2.

Drag a text box onto the stage.

3.

With the text box selected, choose Window| Panels|Text Options to open the Text Options panel. You can also open it by clicking the Show Character button on the lower right beneath the stage and selecting the Text Options tab.

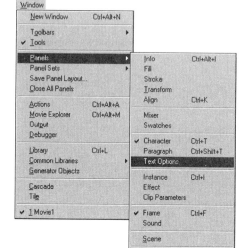

4.

From the drop-down menu, select Input Text. On the stage, the Input text box will have a large square on the bottom-right corner. Static text has the square at the top right.

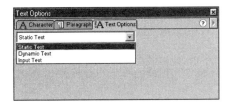

5.

Select Single-Line input, which restricts the entry to a single line. Multiline allows the user to enter a paragraph of text. The Password option displays asterisks on the screen when the user enters text.

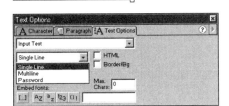

6.

Select the Border/Bg option to add a border around the text, which will create a box in which the user can enter information. The border can also be used simply as a border for text.

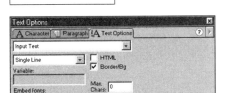

7.

You must also enter a variable name in the Variable field. If you don't, while the user can still change the text on screen, the original text will be redisplayed every time the movie loops back to the start. A variable is a "pretend mailbox" where a user can store information that Flash can pick up later and read. Variables also allow Flash to perform a number of different computations and programming steps.

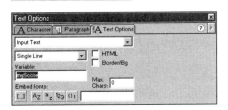

Using Fonts

Using different fonts helps to give your Web page flair and style without the space needed for graphics. To insure a consistent display on all Web browsers, you should stick to one of the common three fonts (_sans, _serif, _typewriter). Flash will match these fonts to those available on the user's browser.

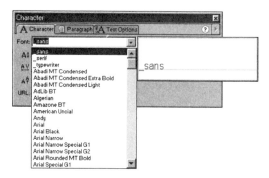

1.

Create a text box anywhere on the stage and type the starting value for the text (for example, "Mary").

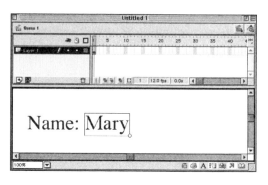

2.

Select the entire text within the text box. The font change will apply to the entire entry.

You can also select your font before you begin typing, if you prefer.

3.

With the text box selected, click the Show Character button to open the Character panel.

4.

Click the Font drop-down menu. Notice that Flash displays sample text for each font as you scroll through the available fonts.

Double-clicking on the text in the text box is an easy way to select the entire field.

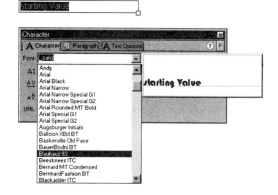

Embedding Fonts

Flash automatically embeds fonts, which can increase file size, so use embedded fonts sparingly. If you need to use a lot of different fonts, you can choose only those characters you need to embed, which will help to reduce the file size.

1.

Create a new text box anywhere on the stage and enter some sample text.

2.

Select the text within the text box.

3.

Open the Text Options panel. Select Input Text from the drop-down menu.

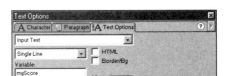

4.

Select the Include Entire Font Outline button to include all of the selected font in the Flash movie.

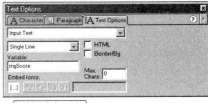

5.

If you know that you will only be using a few letters of this font, you can choose to embed only those letters. Unselect the Include Entire Font Outline button. Copy the letters from the text field and paste them into the empty white input box to the right of the Embed Fonts buttons.

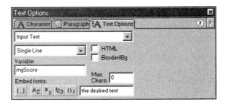

6.

Text can also be formatted in standard HTML. Select the HTML checkbox. This will allow the use of HTML type formatting and the text will be displayed as if in a browser.

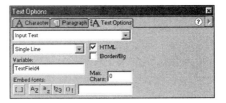

Form Validation

If you create a form, you should also check for errors before the form is submitted. It is helpful to have only correct data submitted, but you need to trade off the programming time against the cost of incorrect data to decide which option is best for your site. You might need to check input for correct type; for example, if you ask for an age, you can check that the user input is a number. You might need to check a number for correct length (as in a phone number), or check if a number is either too big or too small (for example, someone's age should not be –2 or greater than 200).

Character Length

Character length (the number of characters in a string) might be important in the case of phone numbers, zip codes, and social security numbers, to name a few. Flash checks to make sure there are not too many characters in a field but you have to manually check for too few with ActionScript. The following example creates an input text box with character length check.

1.

Create an empty text box. Select Input Text from the Text Options panel, select the Border/Bg option, and input a maximum number of characters in the Max. Chars. window. Name it in the Variable window.

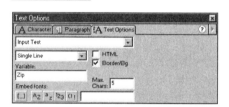

Notice if you test the movie at this point, you can enter information into the text box, but only up to the number of characters you specified.

2.

Create a button as shown, and place it on the main Timeline. This button will check for the appropriate length when clicked.

3.

Attach the following ActionScript to the button. Make sure you replace *TextName* with the name of your text input box and *MaxCharNum* with the number you entered in the Max. Chars. window. The button will now check if the length of the input is smaller than the required number of characters. If the input length is too short, everything in the window is erased. (You can also send a message to the user indicating that they typed in too few characters. This can be done using the dialog box that is covered later in this chapter.)

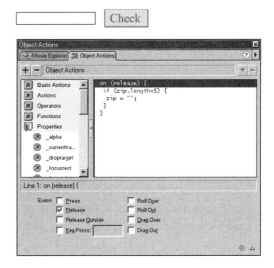

```
on (release){
 if (TextName.length < MaxCharNum){
   TextName = "";
 }
}
```

Character Type Checking

Checking for a specific character type can be just as important as checking for length of input. You might need to make sure that the user types in numbers where you expect numbers and letters where you expect letters.

Check for All Numbers

Create a text box that checks whether a user has input letters in a string of numerals.

1.

Create an empty text box. Select Input Text from the Text Options panel and select the Border/Bg option. Name the text box in the Variable window.

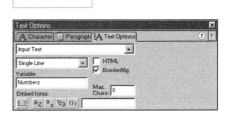

2.

Create a button and place it on the main Timeline. This button will check for the appropriate type when clicked.

3.

Attach the following ActionScript to the button. Replace *TextName* with the name of your text input box. The button will now check that the input entered in the text box contains only numbers, using the built-in Flash function **int**, which converts a string to an integer. If any letters appear in the text box, **int** returns 0; otherwise **int** returns the number. If letters appear in the text box, everything in the box is deleted.

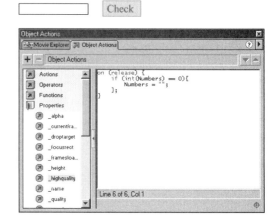

```
on (release) {
  if (int(TextName) == 0){
     TextName = "";
  };
}
```

Check for All Letters

Create a text box that checks whether a user has input numerals in a string of all letters.

1.

Attach the following ActionScript to the button you created in the last exercise. Make sure you replace *TextName* with the name of your text input box. The button now checks if the information typed in the text box by the user is all letters. The ActionScript looks at each letter in the string and tests if it is a number. If the script encounters a number, it stops looking and clears the text box.

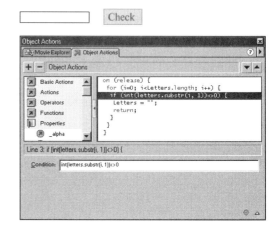

```
on (release) {
  for (i=0; i< TextName.length; i++) {
    if (int(TextName.substr(i, 1))<>0) {
       TextName = "";
       return;
    }
  }
}
```

Minimum and Maximum Validation

Checking for the minimum or maximum of a value can be very important in many forms. You might want to make sure the user has entered a valid age, a valid date, or even a valid year. Validating during the user-entry process (asking the user to fix the invalid information) is much easier than trying to guess what the user meant by an invalid entry.

1.

Create an empty text box. Select Input Text from the Text Options panel and select the Border/Bg option. Name the text box in the Variable window.

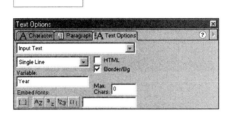

2.

Create a button and place it on the main Timeline. This button will check to ensure the user's input is within an appropriate range of numbers.

3.

Attach the following ActionScript to the button. Replace *TextName* with the name of your text input box. Also replace *Max* with your maximum value and *Min* with your minimum value. The button will check if the information typed in the text box falls between the minimum and maximum values you chose. If the number is greater than the maximum or less than the minimum, the text box is cleared.

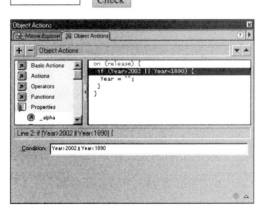

```
on (release) {
 if (TextName >Max || TextName <Min) {
    TextName = "";
 }
}
```

Creating Forms Controls

Web sites can use many different types of standard forms controls: radio buttons, checkbox buttons, drop-down menus, and entry fields, to name a few. Flash does not have any built-in code to do any but the simplest of forms controls.

Checkbox Buttons

Checkbox buttons are standard square buttons that have two states, an *On* state and an *Off* state. The state is shown visually with a check mark. A set of checkboxes can typically have more than one box selected.

1.

Select the Rectangle tool and draw a small unfilled square on the stage. The stroke should be a dark color. This will be the empty or Off state of the button.

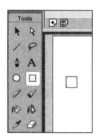

2.

With the square selected, click the Show Info button to open the Info panel.

3.

From the Info panel, select the Stroke tab and select a pixel value of 3 for the stroke, which will give the button a bold, wide edge.

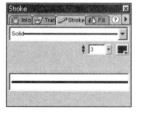

4.

Convert this square into a button symbol. This action will place a reusable button symbol in the movie Library.

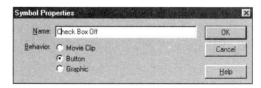

5.

Edit the checkbox button so that it has the same graphic for every state but the Hit state. Because the square is empty, the hit will only be detected at the line of the button and not inside of it. Draw a small square the size of the square box in the Hit state; the color is irrelevant.

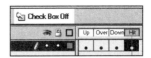

6.

Create the check mark using the Line tool. Set the stroke to 3 pixels, and resize the check mark so it fits easily inside of the square. Copy the check mark from the stage (you will paste it later).

7.

Open the movie Library and duplicate the checkbox button symbol you created in Steps 1 through 4. Give the button a meaningful name (such as Check Box On) to designate that it will be the checked version of the checkbox.

8.

Edit the Check Box On button symbol and add a layer. This layer will contain the check mark. Paste the check mark into the Up state.

9.

Create a new symbol, choosing Movie Clip as its behavior to hold these two buttons.

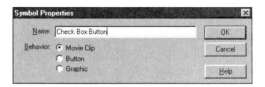

10.

Edit the checkbox button movie clip. Place the Off button in the first frame. Insert a keyframe in Frame 10 (which leaves enough space to read the label that will be attached to the first keyframe). Place the On button in this new keyframe.

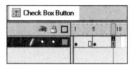

11.

Label both keyframes (the Off state and the On state of the button), which will allow the movie to toggle between the two buttons.

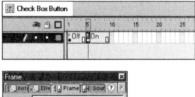

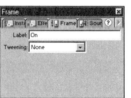

12.

Position the playhead at Frame 1. Select the Off button and attach the following ActionScript:

```
on (release) {
 gotoAndStop ("On");
}
```

Position the playhead to Frame 10. Attach the following ActionScript to the selected On button:

```
on (release) {
 gotoAndStop ("Off");
}
```

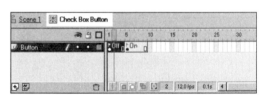

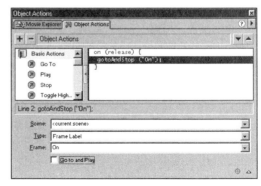

Add a **stop()** command on the first frame of the checkbox movie. This command will en-sure that the movie stops right at the beginning. The button will toggle between the On and Off state each time the user clicks it.

Fields and Labels

Fields with labels are used in forms in which you wish a user to enter information. They can also be used for lengthy text (such as comments) entered by the user. They are very standard and very simple.

1.

Select the Text tool and create an empty text box (it can be single- or multilined).

2.

Select Input Text in the Text Options panel and give the text a border by checking the Border/ Bg box. Give this text box a name (such as User Comments) in the Variable field.

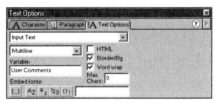

3.

Select the Text tool and enter a label for the text area. Choose Static text. Don't make it select-able. You may use Device fonts if you wish. Place the label on the stage close to the text area.

Dialog Boxes

Dialog boxes are used in many applications. They can give the user a list of items to choose from, or they can simply show a message in a window, such as the error messages that pop up in Windows. In Flash, dialog boxes are best handled with movie clips.

Creating Dialog Boxes

Create a pop-up dialog box with text and a button to close the box when the user is finished reading the message.

1.

Create a movie clip symbol. Give it a meaningful name, such as Dialog Box.

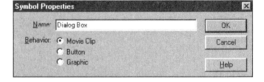

2.

With the Rectangle tool, draw the dialog box area and type in the message text.

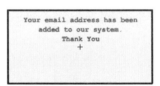

3

Create a new button symbol (to close the dialog box) and place it in the dialog box movie clip.

4.

Attach the following ActionScript to the button. The script will cause the dialog box to disappear from the main Timeline (**_visible = false**) when the button is clicked.

```
on (release) {
 this._visible = false;
}
```

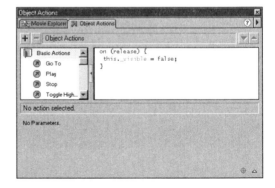

5.

Place the dialog box movie clip in the main Timeline exactly where you want it to pop up on the stage. Give the movie clip instance a name.

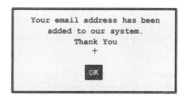

6.

Attach the following ActionScript to the dialog box movie clip. This script will cause the dialog box to not be shown at the start.

```
onClipEvent (load) {
  this._visible = false;
}
```

7.

Create a new button symbol that will cause the dialog box to appear. Attach the following ActionScript to the button, replacing *myInstance* with the name of your movie clip instance. The script will cause the dialog box to pop open each time the button is clicked.

```
on (release) {
  myInstance._visible = true;
}
```

Radio Buttons and Drop-Down Selections

Both radio buttons and drop-down selections are often used in forms. The complex methods to create them are beyond the scope of this book, so we will supply only a brief description of each.

Radio buttons appear in a group of buttons that are related to each other in such a way that only one of the group can be in the On state at a time. Any time a user turns a radio button On, every other radio button turns Off. So each radio button must know the state of all of the others.

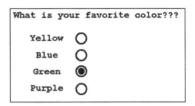

Drop-down selections allow users to select from a list of items. This list of items is hidden until the user clicks to open the list. In most drop-down selections, the chosen selection is displayed in a box, and the list appears directly below the box. The user can opt to select from within the list or close the list without making a selection. The user can make only one selection at a time.

Doing Arithmetic

Some types of entry boxes need to have some arithmetic or calculations done on them for them to be useful. For instance, you wish to keep a count of the number of times a button is clicked and display it to the user. Or the user might enter the weight of a box they wish to ship, and you calculate the cost and display it.

Display Information from Internal Only

You can create dynamic text fields that report information to the user based on internal calculations (the calculations don't require user input).

1.

Create a button and place it on the main Timeline.

2.

Create an empty text box. Select Dynamic Text from the Text Options panel and select the Border/Bg option. Deselect the Selectable checkbox. Name the text box in the Variable window (for example, YesCount).

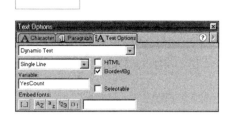

3.

Attach the following ActionScript to the button. Replace *TextName* with the name of your text input box. The script updates the value in the text box by 1 each time the user clicks the button, and displays the total number of times the button is clicked. The ++ in the ActionScript, which increments the value by 1, is the equivalent of **TextName = TextName + 1**.

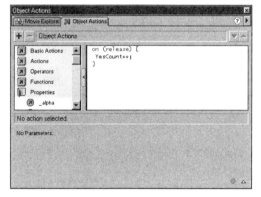

```
on (release) {
  TextName ++;
}
```

Display Information from User Input

This utility takes information from user input then responds and displays information based on that input.

1.

Create a button and place it on the main Timeline.

2.

Create an empty text box. Select Dynamic Text from the Text Options panel and select the Border/Bg option. Deselect the Selectable checkbox. Name the button in the Variable window (for example, Cost). This text box will display the results of calculations.

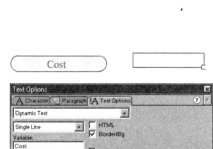

3.

Create empty text boxes that will collect user input for the calculations. Select Input Text from the Text Options panel and select the Border/Bg option. Give each box a different name in the Variable window.

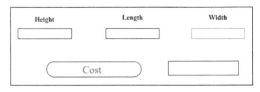

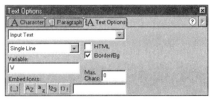

4.

Attach the following ActionScript to the button. Replace *TextName* with the name of your input box. The equation will calculate the area of a box and multiply it by 2 ($2). Replace *Input(1,2,3)* with your user-input text box names. Replace the sample equation to calculate what you want to display on your page.

```
on (release) {
 TextName = Input1*Input2*Input3*2.00;
}
```

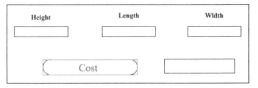

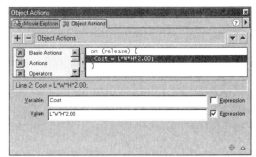

Using Smart Clips

Smart clips are movie clips with brains. Flash 5 comes with a small Library of three smart clips. The Menu smart clip, a drop-down menu that allows users to select from a list of items, is very useful for creating forms. One of the most common ways to ensure correct and consistent data entry is to give the user a list of items from which to select rather than asking them to type their entry.

Any movie clip with ActionScripting in it can be changed into a smart clip so that other developers can reuse the ActionScript without needing to recode it. Smart clips enable a team of developers to share the same code when they need to. Creating your own smart clips is beyond the scope of this book, but you can use any of the three included smart clips in your own movies.

1.

Open the Smart Clips Library (Window|
Common Libraries|Smart Clips).

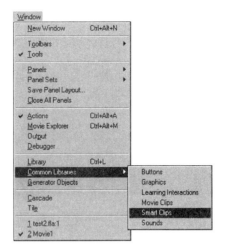

2.

Drag the Menu smart clip onto the stage. Notice that the symbol in the Library for a smart
clip is different than the symbol for a movie
clip.

3.

In order to use the Menu smart clip, you need
to set up your own list of items from which the
user chooses. Select the Menu smart clip on
the stage and open the Smart Clip Parameters
(Window|Panels|Clip Parameters). This list
usually changes with every movie you create.

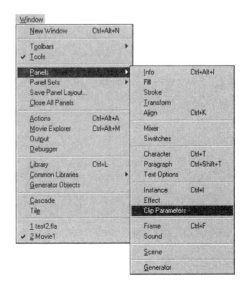

4.

Clip Parameters panel gives a brief description (largely indecipherable unless you are a programmer), in the lower half of the panel, of what the smart clip does. The panel also lists the variables that are used in the smart clip. You cannot change anything in the Name column; those are the variable names determined by the smart clip. In the Menu smart clip, these variables are Items and Style. Items is an *array*, which means that the variable Items has multiple values—as many values as you have items in the list. Style asks you to decide if this menu will work cross-platform (Auto), or only on the Mac or Windows.

5.

Double-clicking on Items|Array[] brings up its Values panel. Double-click each of the Values to enter the items to be included in the drop-down menu. You can add or delete entries by using the + or - buttons at the top of the panel. You can also change the order of the list items by using the up and down arrow buttons at the top of the panel to move entries to a new position.

Each click of an arrow button takes you up or down a step. If you need to move an item more than one position, you need to click and wait for the move to occur before you click the arrow button again. You cannot move multiple steps in a continuous motion.

6.

The smart clip contains all the logic needed to make the list appear on the screen when the user clicks the field. However, the smart clip isn't smart enough to know what to do with the selected item, so you need to tell Flash where to put or display the selection. First, test the movie to make sure you can pick an item from the drop-down list. Shown here is the menu item list box as it looks when the movie runs.

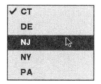

7.

Select the List Value box on the stage and double-click the onClipEvent command in the Actions section of the Object Actions panel. This transfers the command to the right-hand panel.

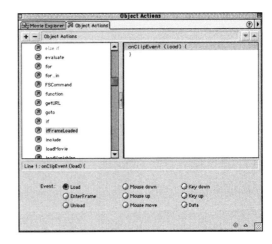

8.

The description in the Parameter Info for the Menu smart clip states that you need to call the onMenu function next. Therefore, with the onClipEvent command still highlighted in the right-hand portion of the Object Actions panel, double-click on the Function command in the left-hand side of the Object Actions panel. The function command is added to the code, but it is not yet complete.

Description:

Paramter Info:
items[] – A dynamic list of text items that you want to appear in your menu structure.

CallBack Summary:

```
// Define the following method in the onLoad() handler.
// OnMenu() will be invoked whenever you select any items
// in the menu.
onClipEvent(load) {
// item - a string in the form "itemXX" where "XX"
// is the item ofset
// label - the text string for the item
function onMenu(item, label) {
//+
// your code goes here
//-
}
}
```

9.

To replace the *Not Yet Seen* warning in the Object Actions panel, enter "onMenu" as the Name of the function. Enter "item,label" (no spaces between them) as the Parameters.

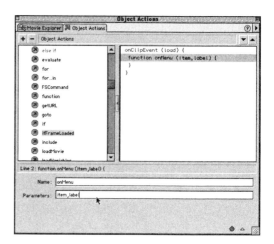

If you are not familiar with programming, a function is a piece of code that performs a task and returns one or more values to the calling program. You can think of a function as a car—you start it up and use it, but you don't have to understand how it works in order to drive it. You don't need to know how a function works to use it, either; you just need to know that parameters are the values that the function returns. In the menu example, because the list contains a group of state names, the function needs to tell you which state the user picked. The Menu smart clip has two parameters: Item holds the number that signifies the position in the list of the user's choice starting from 0 (DE, for example, is the second item on the list; if the user selects it, the variable Item is set to 1). Label holds the text value that the user selected ("DE" in this example).

10.

You can create a dynamic text field to report which item in the list is selected. Though most of your options for handling the user's data is beyond the scope of this book, you can easily create a dynamic variable to test if the list box is working. Type some static text on the stage ("The selected state is:"). Use the Text tool to create a text box that contains dynamic text. You may leave the box empty, but set the variable name to Choice. Deselect the selectable box.

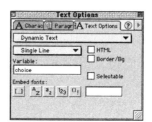

11.

Click on the + button at the top of the Object Actions palette and choose SetVariable from the Actions menu. You still need to enter the specific variable to set.

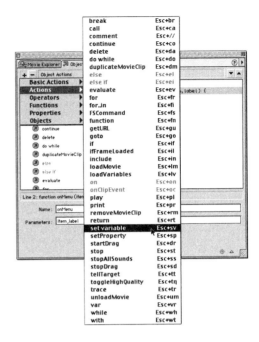

12.

Enter "_level0.choice" for the Variable. Do not select the Expression checkbox. Enter "label" as the Value. This time, you must select the Expression box or else the value will set the letters *LABEL* and not the state name that the variable "label" contains.

You need to reference the variable Choice by prefixing it with _level0 because the variable is on the main movie Timeline, but you are trying to change its value from inside the Menu smart clip (a movie clip).

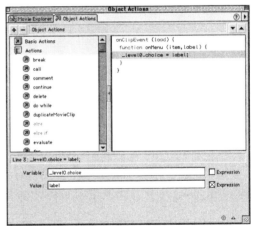

13.

As a final step, press Cmd+Return (Mac) or Ctrl+Enter (Windows) to test the movie.

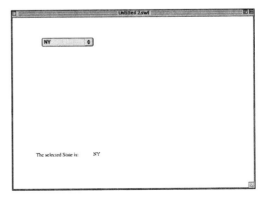

Chapter 9
It's a Wrap

- Perform a test run

- Create a Preloader

- Master the publishing process

- Use projectors and Flash Player

By Jennifer Hall

Test Run

As you create your Flash movie, you need to test it to make sure it works. You could assume that everything is perfect and test it only at the end; however, unless you are an exceptional programmer, the potential for error is high. Also, in Flash, it's best to see how your animation runs as you create it.

Testing Your Movie

Testing the complete movie is simple.

1.

You can play the movie without exporting it. Select Control|Play to step through all the frames in your movie. This process works best to test animations, not to test complicated scripting. Stepping through each frame lets you see transitions slowly. Select Control|Step Forward (.) to move the playhead one frame forward. Select Control|Step Backward (,) to move the playhead one frame back. Rewind the movie with Control|Rewind.

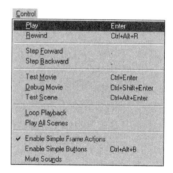

2.

Save your movie. You can test it without saving it, but it's safer to save first.

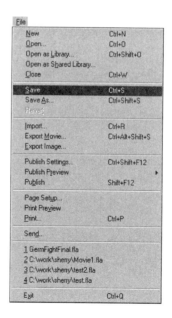

3.

Test your movie. Select Control|Test Movie. In some cases, you will need to enable the frame and/or button actions when testing your movie. Select Control|Enable Simple Buttons to turn on button actions or Control|Enable Simple Frame Actions to test ActionScript in frames.

Testing Scenes

In many cases, your movie will have more than one scene, but you may want to test just one scene without sitting through others.

1.

Select the scene you want to test, using either the Scene panel (Window|Panels|Scene) or the Edit Scene button.

2.

Test the scene by selecting Control|Test Scene.

Using the Bandwidth Profiler

Because your movie is for the Web, you should know how long the movie takes to download. The Bandwidth Profiler gives you that information and shows you what areas in your movie take the longest to download.

1.

To view the Bandwidth Profiler, the movie must be running. Start your movie by selecting Control|Test Movie.

2.

While the movie is playing, select the bandwidth speed from the Debug menu for which you would like to optimize your movie (for example, 28.8).

You must press Enter to start a movie again after you select a different speed.

3.

You can also customize the modem settings used in the test. To do this, select Debug|Customize. Flash lets you create three settings.

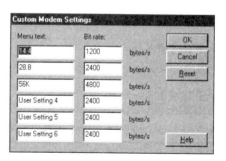

4.

Select View|Bandwidth Profiler so you can watch the results.

5.

The left side of the Bandwidth Profiler shows general information about your movie, the setting that you have selected to test, and the current state of the movie—the frame and how much is loaded. The right side is a graphical representation of the movie. Bars above the red line indicate a point where your movie will bog down when loading at the test speed.

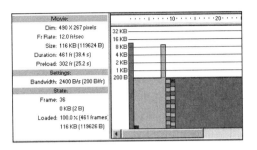

6.

You can view the Bandwidth Profiler in two ways: streaming and frame by frame. For streaming, select View|Streaming Graph. The Timeline at the top now shows seconds; this view illustrates the time each frame takes to download. Notice the alternating light and dark gray boxes—each represents a frame. Any color that is spread out over more than one line will take longer than 1 second to download.

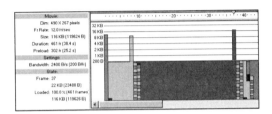

7.

As the movie is streaming, you can view a progress bar that compares how the graphics download compared to how the movie plays. Select View|Show Streaming. The movie will start playing, and you can watch the green bar at the top as your movie loads and the playback marker as the movie plays.

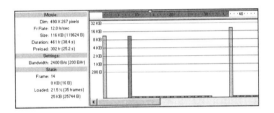

8.

To view the Bandwidth Profiler frame by frame, select View|Frame By Frame Graph. This graph presents a single bar for each frame; the scale at the top is in frames. Any frame above the red line will take longer to load.

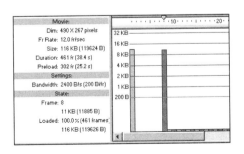

9.

To get a printed version of this information, you must generate a size report. From the main Flash environment (not the Flash Player), select File|Publish Settings. Select the Flash tab and check the Generate Size Report button to create a report in the same directory as your movie called MovieName Report.txt.

```
ants Report.txt - Notepad
File  Edit  Search  Help   Send
Movie Report
-------------
Frame #      Frame Bytes      Total Bytes     Page
-------      -----------      -----------     ----------------
   1            12365            12365         Scene 1
   2                2            12367           2
   3                2            12369           3
   4                2            12371           4
   5                2            12373           5
   6                2            12375           6
   7                2            12377           7
   8            11885            24262           8
   9               16            24278           9
  10               16            24294          10
  11               16            24310          11
  12               16            24326          12
  13               16            24342          13
  14               16            24358          14
  15               16            24374          15
  16               16            24390          16
  17               16            24406          17
  18               16            24422          18
  19               17            24439          19
  20               17            24456          20
  21               17            24473          21
  22               17            24490          22
  23               17            24507          23
  24               17            24524          24
  25               17            24541          25
  26               17            24558          26
  27               17            24575          27
```

Optimizing Your Movie

You need to optimize your movie for every bandwidth, though it is probably not possible for the movie to play smoothly for very low bandwidths. Flash's online documentation contains a checklist to optimize playback at any speed. Remember, your movie won't play faster than it was designed for, even at high bandwidths.

The online checklist (Help|Using Flash: Publishing and Exporting/Optimizing Movies) covers using symbols, tweened animations, movie clips, and MP3 sound to optimize speed; it also suggests processes to avoid (animating bitmaps and overuse of line types, fonts, and gradients).

Creating a Preloader

A Preloader entertains the user as the movie loads and prevents delays when the user views the main movie. Although they're nice, Preloaders can also bog down, so stick with simple graphics. You can create a Preloader in two ways: by manipulating graphics and with ActionScript.

Creating a Preloader with Graphics

Using a graphic Preloader loads all the movie's graphics—they're all placed on the stage during the Preloader scene. If the graphics take a long time to load, the Preloader takes longer and the user has to wait. This method does not use any code.

1.

Add a scene to hold your Preloader (Insert|Scene). Name it Preloader and make sure it is the first scene to play (Window| Panels|Scene).

2.

For this process, you need a full-screen background. The other graphics will load behind the full-screen graphic. Make a large rectangle that covers the whole stage or use an existing background from the movie you're preloading.

3.

Make sure this scene has few graphics: for example, use a slider bar (tweened) or a spinning object. Add a layer above the background layer for the progress bar. Create a small rectangle (taller than wide) for the progress bar and make it a symbol. Place it in the progress bar layer.

4.

Insert a keyframe at Frame 30 on the progress bar layer. Scale the progress bar lengthwise to show what it will look like when loading is finished. Tween between the starting progress bar (which should be small) and the ending progress bar.

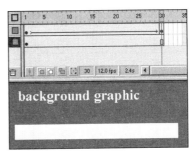

5.

Add a layer below the background layer. All the graphics, including sounds, will be placed in this layer. Space out the loading process, adding more frames to the movie if you need to. Start loading graphics at Frame 2 (insert a keyframe). Add a keyframe every other frame, adding about five graphics at each new keyframe. To see what you're doing, turn off visibility on the other layers. The placement of the graphics doesn't matter—they're behind the background.

6.

If you have any sounds, load them near the end. You need to turn off sound during the preload. Select the frame that the sound is in and open the Sound panel (Window| Panels|Sound). In the Sync drop-down menu select Stop. The sound won't play during preload but will be loaded into memory.

Creating a Preloader with ActionScript

This method keeps a movie in a particular loop until the entire scene is loaded. To use this method, you need to create a loop of code and test for complete loading.

1.

Add a scene (Insert|Scene) named Preloader, and make sure it is the first scene to play (Window|Panels|Scene).

2.

A rotating figure works best for this method. Create a graphic symbol that is not a circle. Create a new movie clip and place the graphic in it. Insert a keyframe after Frame 5. With the first frame selected, open the Frame panel (Window|Panels|Frame). Set Tweening to Motion. Set the Rotate field to CW (clockwise) or CCW (counterclockwise) and Times to more than 1. The Times field determines how fast the graphic rotates. Place the Rotation movie clip on the main Timeline in the Preloader scene.

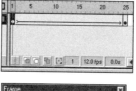

3.

Create a button for the user to click when preloading is finished. Add another layer for the button and place the button after Frame 5. You need a couple of keyframes to do the rotation and to loop in the ActionScript. This button appears only when the movie is loaded.

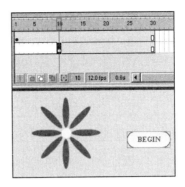

4.

The button jumps the movie to the next scene. With the button on the stage selected, open the Actions panel (Window|Actions). Make sure the tab says Object Actions, not Frame Actions. (If it says Frame Actions, select the button on the stage.) From the Basic Actions, double-click On Mouse Event, with the checkbox in the parameters section set to Release. Then double-click Go To. For Scene, enter the scene you wish to go to. When the button is released, the movie goes to the first frame of the selected scene.

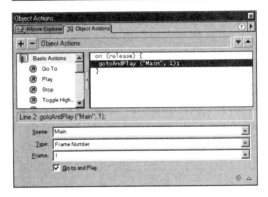

5.

Now you'll create the Preloader ActionScript. It's best to keep all the script on one layer, primarily so you can find it. Add a layer and a keyframe in the frame where the button first appears. Open the Frame Actions panel. From the Basic Actions, select Stop.

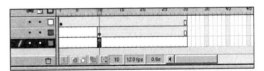

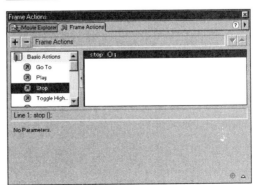

6.

Insert a keyframe at Frame 2 to check that the next scene is loaded. In the Frame Actions panel, select If Frame Is Loaded. Set Scene to the next scene and set Frame to the last frame of the next scene. The script tests whether everything up to that point is loaded.

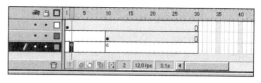

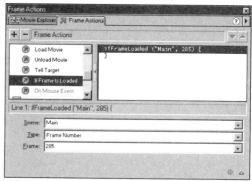

7.

Select the IfFrameLoaded line, then select the Go To command. You are going to jump to the button. Set Scene to <current scene> and Frame to the frame number where the button first appears. Make sure the Go To And Play box is *not* checked.

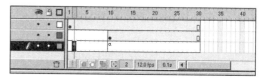

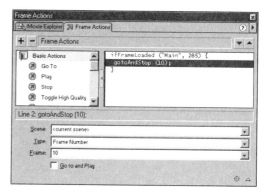

8.

Now you create the loop that keeps the movie in the Preloader until the next section is loaded. Insert a keyframe right before the button, in the ActionScript layer. Open the Frame Actions panel and select Go To. Set Scene to <current scene> and Frame to Frame 1. Make sure the Go To And Play box *is* checked. The movie will loop to the beginning each time it gets to this frame and perform the preload test again. Test this movie.

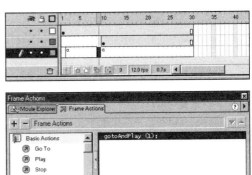

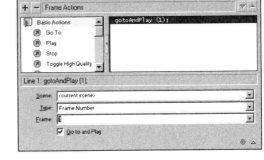

The Publishing Process

Publishing is the final part of creating a movie, where you get to see all your hard work pay off—and let everyone else see it, too.

Using the Publish Settings Box

In this box, you tweak how the final movie looks and runs. You can put the movie out in many different formats: Flash, HTML, an image (GIF, JPEG, PNG), a Windows or Macintosh projector, or a QuickTime or RealPlayer movie. You can also change the settings for each format.

1.

Open the Publish Settings box (File|Publish Settings). Click the Formats tab to select which format you want to use.

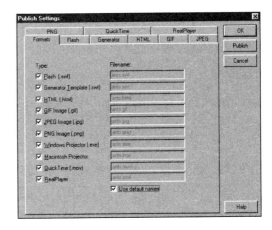

2.

Default names of published files are based on the name of the Flash movie. Change a name by unchecking the Use Default Names box.

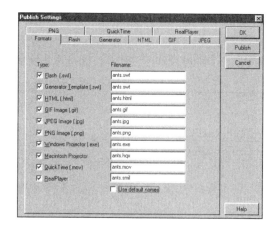

Publish Preview

Once you've completed the settings in the Publish Settings box, you can publish your movie. Clicking the Publish button from the Publish Settings box publishes in all the types. You can also publish just one type at a time by selecting File|Publish Preview and choosing a file type.

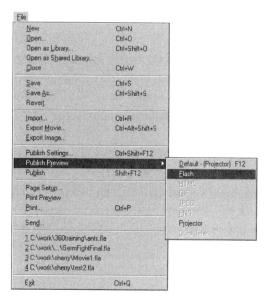

HTML

The HTML publish setting creates a very basic Web page with just enough HTML code to display the Flash movie.

The Automatic Approach

This approach uses the default settings for the HTML final Web page. It is assumed that you will edit the HTML code after the movie is published.

1.

At the Publish Settings dialog box, first make sure the HTML box is checked. Then select the HTML tab. The default settings display.

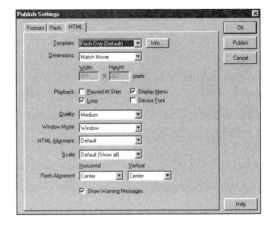

2.

Select a template from the pull-down menu. Clicking the Info button brings up a template description and other requirements. For example, the Image Map template requires selecting GIF, JPEG, or PNG.

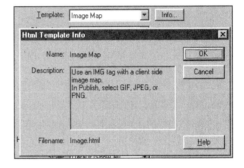

3.

The Dimensions selection lets you decide the size of the Flash movie in the final Web page. If you select Match Movie, you cannot change anything because the size is fixed to the size of the movie document in the Flash authoring environment.

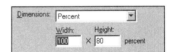

4.

The Playback options are fairly self-explanatory. Paused At Start means the Flash movie will start only when the user starts it. Display Menu creates a playback options menu when the user right-clicks (Windows) or Ctrl+clicks (Macintosh) the movie. Loop starts the movie over at the beginning when the last frame is reached. Device Font uses antialiased fonts whenever a movie contains fonts not found on the end user's browser.

5.

The Quality option changes the ratio between the quality of the images and the movie's speed. In order of descending high quality/low playback speed to low quality/high playback speed, the Quality options are as follows:

- *Best*—antialiasing on; bitmaps smoothed

- *High*—antialiasing on; bitmaps smoothed only if there is no animation

- *Medium*—some antialiasing; bitmaps not smoothed

- *Auto High*—antialiasing on unless speed drops below a target fps value

- *Auto Low*—antialiasing off in most cases

- *Low*—antialiasing always off

6.

The Window Mode selection affects only Internet Explorer 4 or later. It allows the Flash movie to play with a transparent background.

7.

HTML Alignment sets where the Flash movie will be displayed on the HTML page. The default values are Centered and Centered. The Left, Top, Right, and Bottom options align the corresponding edge of the movie with the appropriate edge of the browser window and crops the movie as needed.

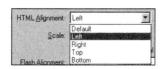

8.

The Scale option rescales the movie when height and width are changed. Default (Show All) rescales without distortion. If the specified area is bigger than the original movie dimensions, borders are added. No Border rescales with no distortion and no borders, but the movie might be cropped. Exact Fit rescales the movie without cropping, but distortion might occur.

9.

Flash Alignment aligns the Flash movie within the Flash Player. Default settings are Center for both Horizontal and Vertical alignments.

10.

Selecting the Show Warning Messages checkbox displays messages to the Flash designer if some of the HTML tags conflict.

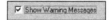

Using Templates and Hand Coding

With this approach, Flash uses templates to create the HTML page. Each time you modify the Publish settings, the resulting HTML page uses the selected template with the settings to create a Web page. Any template you create must be located in the Flash 5/HTML folder.

1.

Use any HTML editor to create or edit a template. To use default values, leave the variables empty. The list of template parameters and values can be found in the Flash 5 documentation that ships with the software. After you have modified the template, save it to the HTML folder. In the Publish Settings dialog box, select the appropriate template.

2.

If you are experienced with HTML, you can edit or create an HTML document to display a Flash movie. The HTML code must use OBJECT (Internet Explorer) and EMBED (Netscape Navigator). OBJECT has four settings: HEIGHT, WIDTH, CLASSID, and CODEBASE. All other parameters appear inside PARAM tags. The EMBED tag has four settings: HEIGHT, WIDTH, QUALITY, and LOOP. To use both tags, position the EMBED tag just before closing the OBJECT tag. The Flash 5 documentation lists tags used in the Publish Settings dialog box.

Alternate Images

Although in most cases you want the user to see the actual Flash movie you have created, sometimes it is nice to give the unplugged user a taste of what is displayed. The Publish Settings dialog box lets you publish a GIF, a JPEG, a PNG, an animated GIF, or a QuickTime movie.

GIF and Animated GIF

Flash exports the first frame of the movie as a GIF unless you mark an alternate keyframe with the label #Static. Flash optimizes an animated GIF, storing only the frame-to-frame changes. It also exports the entire movie unless you specify a range of frames with the labels #First and #Last.

Open the Publish Settings dialog box and make sure the GIF box is checked. Select the GIF tab. These are the default settings for the standard GIF. For an animated GIF, select the Animated radio button. You can then select whether and how many times to loop.

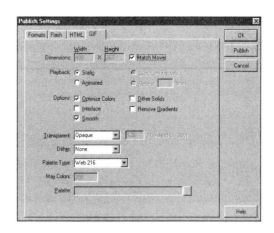

JPEG

JPEG format lets you publish an image as a highly compressed, 24-bit bitmap. GIF is generally better for exporting line art than JPEG, and JPEG is good for images. Flash exports the first frame of the movie as a JPEG unless you mark an alternate keyframe with the label #Static.

Open the Publish Settings dialog box and make sure the JPEG box is checked. Select the JPEG tab. These are the default settings for the standard JPEG.

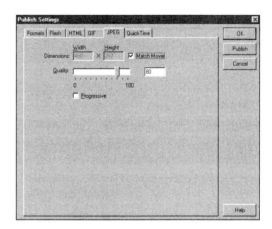

PNG

PNG is the only cross-platform bitmap that supports transparency. Flash exports the first frame of the movie as a PNG unless you mark an alternate keyframe with the label #Static.

Open the Publish Settings dialog box and make sure the PNG box is checked. Select the PNG tab. These are the default settings for the standard PNG.

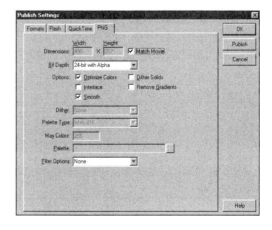

QuickTime 4

QuickTime creates movies in the standard QuickTime 4 player. The Flash movie plays exactly as it does in the Flash Player, retaining all its interactivity. This is a nice way to create a QuickTime movie with controls other than the standard.

Open the Publish Settings dialog box, and make sure the QuickTime box is checked. Select the QuickTime tab. These are the default settings for QuickTime.

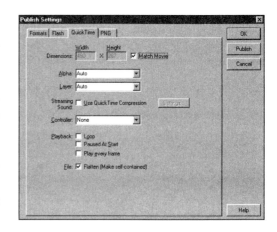

Projectors

Projectors are standalone Flash movies that an end user can run without the Flash plug-in or the Flash Player (the Flash Player is covered in detail later in this chapter). The only drawback is that the projector is platform dependent; therefore, you need to create a projector for both Macintosh and Windows systems.

1.

Open the Publish Settings dialog box and make sure the Windows Projector, the Macintosh Projector, or both checkboxes are checked.

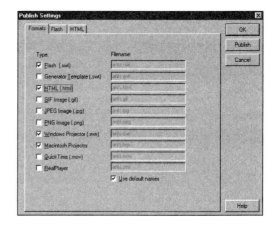

2.

When a projector is created, the Flash Player is included in the projector, so when you run the projector, it looks just like the movie is running in the Flash Player.

3.

You can also create a projector from the standalone Flash Player (File|Create Projector); however, this option creates a projector only for the system you are currently running in.

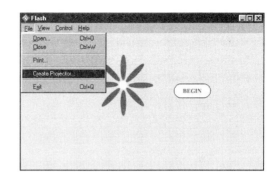

Full-Screen Mode

One of the advantages of creating a projector is that you can run the movie in full-screen mode. Your movie will display across the whole screen. You need to make sure the dimensions are proportional to the screen; otherwise, your movie will be distorted.

1.

Open the movie you want to run in full-screen mode. Select a keyframe in Frame 1 of the first scene. Open the Actions panel (Windows|Actions) and make sure the tab is labeled Frame Actions.

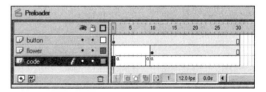

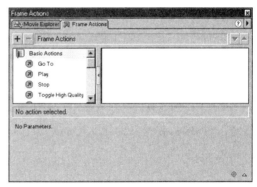

2.

From the Basic Actions, select FSCommand (the full-screen command). The parameters section has a drop-down menu, Commands For Standalone Player, that contains all the commands you can use with FSCommand. Fullscreen makes the movie full screen, Allowscale scales the movie to fill the screen, Showmenu lets you hide or show the menu bar at the top, and Quit attaches to a button that lets the user quit full-screen mode gracefully.

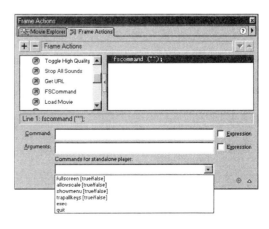

3.

From the drop-down menu, select Fullscreen (True/False). The parameters are filled in automatically and the full screen is automatically set to True. Publish the movie.

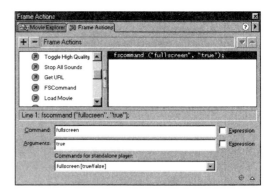

4.

The resulting projector takes over the whole screen. You can zoom in or out of the projector. Because it uses vector graphics, zooming in creates little or no distortion. Esc takes you out of the full-screen viewing again.

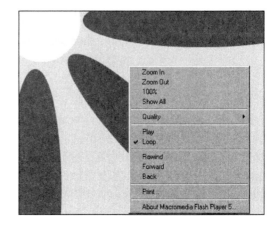

Flash Player

Finally, you can publish your movie using the Flash Player, a standalone player that installs with Flash.

1.

Open the Publish Settings dialog box and make sure the Flash checkbox is checked. Select the Flash tab to view the options.

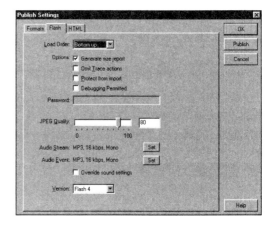

2.

The Load Order drop-down menu determines how Flash draws the first frame. The Top Down setting tells Flash to display the top layer first. The Bottom Up setting does the opposite.

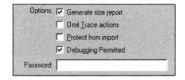

3.

The Generate Size Report option generates a text file that shows information about when a graphic is loaded, how big it is, and how much data each frame contains. Omit Trace Actions helps debug your ActionScript. If you have used trace actions to debug, you disable them by unchecking this box. Protect From Import prevents users from obtaining your .swf file and converting it back into a Flash movie. Debugging Permitted lets users debug even more of the ActionScript and turns on the use of the debugger; you can require users to provide a password.

4.

JPEG Quality controls compression, and thus quality. Setting JPEG compression to 0 provides for the most compression and the lowest quality, because JPEG loses data. This setting applies only to bitmaps. Also note that Flash does not apply this compression to any imported GIFs.

5.

Flash handles sound files in two different ways: event sound and streaming sound. The sound's Sync setting determines which way Flash handles it. An event sound is completely downloaded before it starts playing, whereas a streaming sound plays as it downloads. For each type of sound, Flash gives you settings to tweak. You can also set compression for individual sounds in their properties or choose to override sound settings.

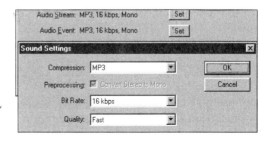

6.

You can determine what version of Flash you would like the output in. Note that if you want to export your Flash movie to an older version, you cannot use any of the newer version's features.

Other Export Formats

You can also export the movie or frames of the movie using the Export Movie feature. With this feature, you can export the movie to a still-image format and create a numbered image file for each frame of the movie. You can also export the sound in a movie using the Export Movie feature and selecting the WAV file format.

1.

Open the Export Movie box (File|Export Movie). Many options are available to export your movie, including Flash Player, QuickTime, Windows AVI, Animated GIF, WAV Audio, EMF Sequence, Bitmap Sequence, and JPEG Sequence.

2.

Export Image exports the current frame of the movie or a selected image. Open the Export Movie box (File|Export Image). Many export formats are available, and many give you further options to set. The Adobe Illustrator format is perfect for exchanging graphics because it is recognized by many drawing applications. Bitmap creates bitmaps from your vector images. Enhanced Metafile is a graphics format for Windows that saves both the vector and bitmap information. PICT is the standard graphics file for the Macintosh.

Configuring Your Server

For your Flash movie to be viewed by the user, the Web server it is on must be configured to recognize the movie as a Flash movie. You must configure the MIME (Multipart Internet Mail Extension) types for the server to correlate the Flash extension (.swf) with Flash.

If your server is administered through an Internet service, contact the service and request that they add the MIME type application/x-shockwave-flash with the extension .swf. If you administer your own server, add the MIME type application/x-shockwave-flash with the extension .swf. The intricacies of server administration are beyond the scope of this book, and will not be covered here.

Part II
Projects

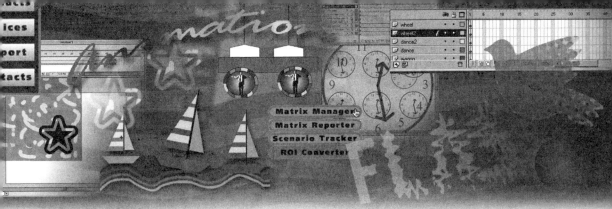

Chapter 10
Drawing

Project 1: Add a gradient fill to logo text

Project 2: Create artwork with Flash's drawing tools

Project 3: Prepare your home page in Flash

By Dan London

Drawing 101: Trying It Out

In Chapters 1, 2, and 3, you learned about Flash's drawing tools and how to structure a movie by using Library elements. Now it's your turn to produce something. In this chapter you'll be working with Flash's drawing tools to create a company's logo. You'll turn simple text into a graphic that will become the centerpoint of your design.

This chapter will also teach you how to lay out a home page for your Web site and discuss several issues that come with it. Though file size and functionality are not specific concerns for this chapter, you should always keep them in mind when preparing content for the Web.

Project 1: Filling Up with Gradients

You have been hired to create a logo for a company called Two Worlds. The two colors for this logo are green and blue. Green represents the world of land and blue represents the world of water: two colors for two worlds. The contrast of the blue and the green will create a distinctive look and feel for this company.

Let's start the logo with the company name and apply a gradient fill to it.

1.

Activate the Text tool by clicking the Text icon or typing "T" on your keyboard. Once your cursor has turned into the symbol that represents the Text tool, click anywhere on the stage.

Because we are creating text that will be part of a logo, it doesn't matter where on the stage you create the text.

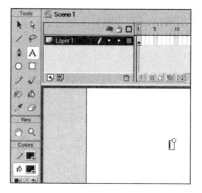

2.

With the text tool activated, type "TWO WORLDS" (in capital letters). Name this layer Text.

3.

Choose the font and size of your logo. Select Window|Panels|Character (or Ctrl+T).

For this example, I chose GlaserSteD. (If you don't have this font, you can use any similar font—in this exercise, the technique is important; the shape of the font really is not.) With the text selected, return to the Character palette, click the drop-down tool for font size, and select 20. You can also select the current size and change it to 20.

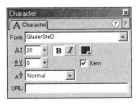

Although you can choose font type and size in the Text menu, you can't see samples of the fonts. Also within the Text menu you can choose only from the default settings listed there.

4.

Select the Arrow tool and click once on the text. Open the Modify menu and choose Break Apart, or press Cmd/Ctrl+B. This will change the text into a vector graphic. Although you can no longer edit the text, you can apply a color gradient.

5.

With the text graphic selected, open the Fill palette and select Radial Gradient from the drop-down menu. Select the slider on the left. Choose a green as your first color. Click the slider on the right, open the Color palette, and chose a blue. Your text should now have the gradient applied through it.

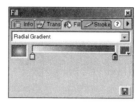

Now that you have created a new gradient, it will appear in your Fill color palette as a selectable choice. It will continue to appear, but only in this movie.

6.

Choose the Paint Bucket tool. Two choices appear below the fill options. Click the icon on the right, which is the Transform Fill tool. With this tool selected, click the TWO WORLDS text.

7.

You can now edit this fill. Center, left, and right points will appear. You can move the center point, stretch the fill across the text, or rotate the fill. Drag the circle that appears across the text and rotate until you get the desired effect.

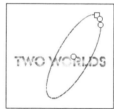

Project 2: Running in Circles

Now that you have created text for your logo, you can create additional artwork with Flash's drawing tools. Flash's native drawing tools give you the advantage of vector editing with raster graphics convenience.

1.

Click the Stroke Color icon and choose the blue used in the previous project. You can choose the color either in the toolbar or by selecting Window|Panels|Stroke. Make sure the stroke style is a solid line and the size is 1 point.

Activate the Rectangle tool (press R) and change the fill color to Transparent.

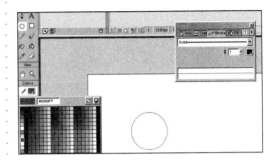

2.

Open a new layer (choose Insert|Layer or press the Insert Layer icon at the bottom left of the Timeline window). Call this layer circle_blue.

Activate the Oval tool (press O). While holding down the Shift key, create a circle on the stage. Activate the Stroke Color icon and click the circle. It should now be blue.

3.

Select the circle with the Arrow tool and open the Info panel. Change both the height and the width to 65.5.

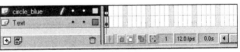

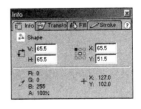

4.

Create a new layer and call it circle_green. Activate circle_blue and copy it. Paste the circle onto the layer you just created and click the circle_green layer.

Change the stroke color to the green you used in the previous project. Now you should have a green circle.

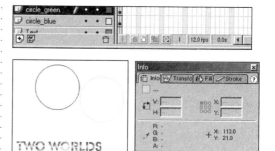

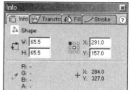

5.

Open the Info palette again and select the blue circle. Change the blue circle's X-Y axis to 291,157. Select the green circle. Change its X-Y axis to 272,145. In the Layers palette, drag the circle_green layer above the circle_blue layer.

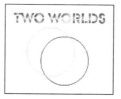

6.

Click your text layer and drag the text so that it sits about 10 pixels above the top of the blue circle.

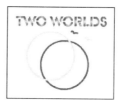

7.

Insert a new layer and call it Birds. Activate the Pencil tool and change the pencil options to Smooth. Change the fill color to the same blue that you used for the circle. Draw a small line-art bird, the V type that might appear in a child's drawing. Copy this bird and paste the copy a little below and to the right of the blue bird. Change the second bird's color to green. Save this movie as twoworlds.fla.

Project 3: Layin' It on the Line

Now that your text logo has been created, it's time to use it. In this project, you'll create the layout of a home page. In this way, you will begin to understand how you prepare individual elements of a Web site for use in Flash 5.

You can download the artwork you will need for this project as well as the example home page layout from the *Flash 5 Visual Insight* ftp site (**ftp.coriolis.com** in the Public/Flash5VI folder).

1.

Start a new movie and name it layout.fla by choosing File|Save.

Select Modify|Movie or press Ctrl+M. Change the width and height to 600×450. Click the Background Color option and choose black as your new background color.

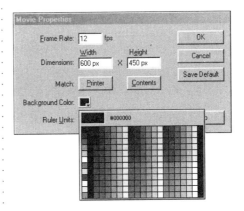

2.

Open your saved twoworlds.fla movie. Select all of the logo by dragging a marquee around it. With the logo selected, press the F8 key or choose Insert|Convert to Symbol.

Name the symbol twoworlds_logo and choose Graphic as its behavior. Save and close the movie.

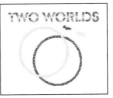

Now the Two Worlds logo is a unified symbol that can be used in as many movies as desired.

3.

Return to the layout.fla movie. Select File|Open as Shared Library and choose twoworlds.fla. The twoworlds_logo should now appear in your Library palette.

If the Library palette is not visible, type Ctrl+L or select Window|Library.

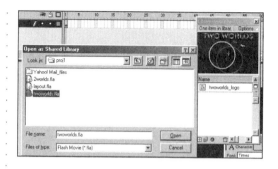

4.

Change the name of Layer 1 to Logo. Select twoworlds_logo from the Library palette by clicking it. Drag an instance of it onto the stage. Place it in the upper-left corner so it matches the example home page layout.

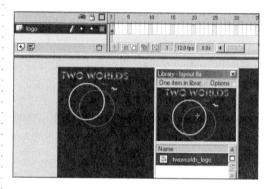

5.

Select File|Import|Images and choose button.png (or press Ctrl+R). When the dialog box opens, make sure Flatten Image is selected, as well as Include Images. Click OK. A green button image named button should now appear in your library.

Create a new layer by selecting Insert|Layer or clicking the + sign on the toolbar at the bottom of the Timeline window. Name this layer company_bt. Select button from the Library palette and drag an instance of it onto the stage. Press F8 or Insert|Convert to Symbol and name it green_button. For its behavior, chose Button.

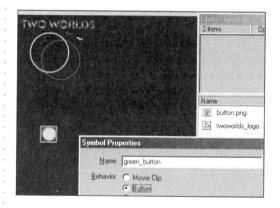

Take another look at the example home page layout. The green button is used five times. Because you converted the button into a symbol, the layout can contain five instances of the green_button symbol instead of five separate graphics. Besides cutting down the file size, converting the button means the computer needs to download it only once.

6.

Create a new layer for the menu bar and name it blue_bar. Select the Fill tool and choose Transparent. Select the Stroke tool and choose the blue from the logo. Open the Stroke panel (Window|Panels|Stroke) and choose 3 as the thickness. Select the Oval tool; while holding down the Shift key, draw a circle that is slightly less than half the height of the movie.

You could import this image as a bitmap, but it's easy enough to create in Flash. Drawing in Flash cuts down on file size, because vector graphics are compressed into smaller files than imported bitmap graphics are.

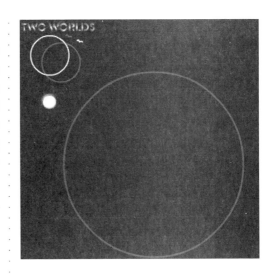

7.

Choose the Arrow tool and draw a box around 50 percent of the blue circle. Cut your selection (Edit|Cut or Cmd/Ctrl+X). Select the remaining half of the circle and place it under and slightly to the left of the Two Worlds logo. With the blue_bar layer selected, press F8 and convert it into a graphics symbol. Name it blue_bar.

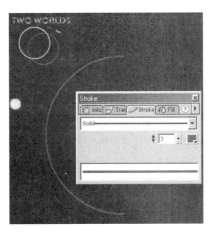

8.

Drag the company_bt layer above the blue_bar layer. Select the green button and place it near the top of the blue bar so it matches the example home page layout.

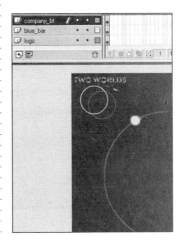

9.

Right-click the green button and choose Edit. You will see the editing window for the company_bt symbol. You'll see choices for Up, Over, Down, and Hit. For this project, you will work only with the Up property.

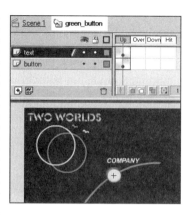

Rename Layer 1 company_bt. Create a new layer named Text. Select the Text tool and click slightly above and to the left of the button. Choose Arial, size 12, with white as the color. Also choose bold and italics. Type "Company". Click the Scene 1 tab to exit the symbol window.

By combining the button and the text into one layer, you have created a symbol that can be affected by mouse clicks on either the button or the text. This feature will come in handy when the time comes to plan rollovers and other mouse events. Though we do not cover mouse behavior in this project, this method will be helpful later in the book.

10.

In this step, you create four more instances of the button symbol named news_bt, invest_bt, present_bt, and future_bt.

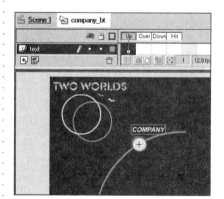

Within the library, right-click on the company_bt symbol and choose Duplicate from the drop-down menu. Give the symbol the name of the button you're creating. From the library, right-click your new button symbol and chose Edit. Click the Company text and type the name of your new button.

Repeat this step for the three remaining buttons.

11.

Create new layers for each of your new buttons (see Step 9). Once you create and name the layer, drag the matching button onto the stage and place it in position (see the example home page layout).

Right-click the news button and choose Edit In Place. Click the text to select it. Move the text to sit left of the bar. Return to your scene by clicking the Scene 1 tab and repeat this step for the remaining buttons.

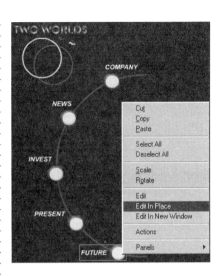

12.

Create a new layer and call it blue_text. Select File|Import and choose blue_text.png from the folder you downloaded for this chapter. Place the image to the right of the blue bar and center it so it matches the example home page layout. Select it and hit F8 or Insert|New Symbol. Name it blue_text. Your logo is now ready for your Web site.

Don't be fooled by the fact this graphic is made up of text; it is still a bitmapped graphic and Flash will treat it as such. The text is not editable.

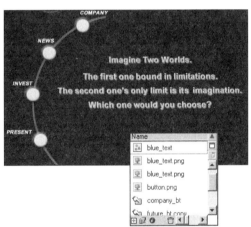

Flash 5 Studio

*The following pages contain
color examples of some of
the projects and techniques
presented in this book.*

Unlocked gradient

Gradient locked before fill

Locking a gradient fill creates a "virtual" color gradient across the image. All objects take on the gradient color "behind" them rather than the using the entire range of the gradient. (Cows are from the Art Parts collection.)

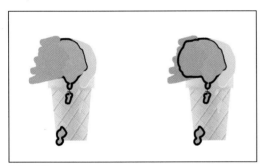

Paints Fills

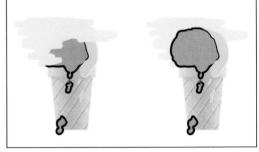

Paints Behind

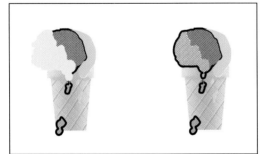

Paints Selection

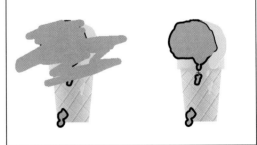

Paints Inside

You can set the Paintbrush tool to four modes in addition to Normal.

Minimum Area: 20
Color Threshold: 50

Minimum Area: 100
Color Threshold: 50

Curve Fit: Pixels

Curve Fit: Very Smooth

Corner Threshold: Many Corners

Corner Threshold: Few Corners

Painting with bitmap fill

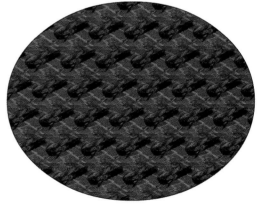

Filling with skewed bitmap fill

Flash gives you many options when you break apart an imported bitmapped image. You can change it to a vector by tracing it, or you can use it as a fill when you paint or fill an object.

Change symbols by adding effects.

3 instances; no effects added

Brightness Effect of +45%

Editing one instance of a symbol changes all instances.

Tint Effects, purple tint at 65%

You can create unlinked symbols then swap them with the original symbols on the stage.

Advanced Effect

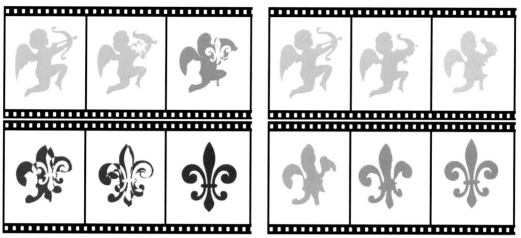

Shape tween with no Shape Hints

Shape tween with one Shape Hint

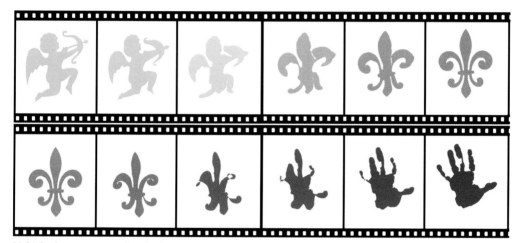

Multiple shape tweens with multiple Shape Hints for each section of the tween

Flash lets you create shape tweens that meld one shape into another when the animation is played.

Moving (left) and Static (right) masks can create exciting animations.

Masked animation shows light traveling though a piece of text.

Timeline with Layer 1 shows the base image.

Layer 2 (masked layer) contains the same text colored gold.

Layer 3 contains the mask that animates to reveal different portions of the gold text.

Create a texture and place an object on top of it as a mask.

Move the texture and allow the mask to remain still.

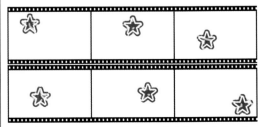

Make the animation a movie clip symbol then animate the textured object across the stage.

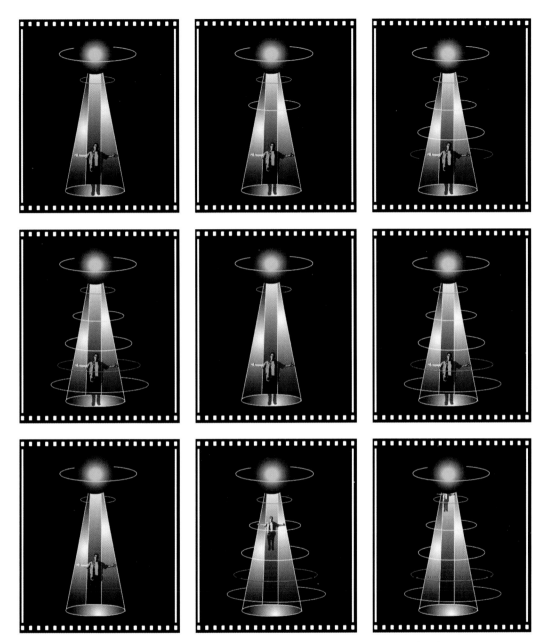

This animation project from Chapter 12 teaches you how to copy and paste keyframes to save time as you create this amusing look at someone vanishing inside an alien spaceship. You'll also create motion tweens and learn to add frames and keyframes to animations.

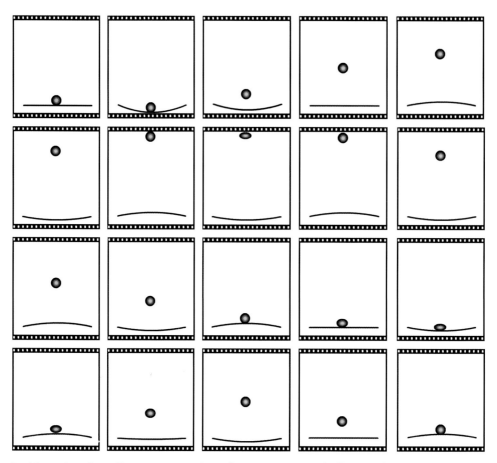

In this project from Chapter 11, you learn how to animate a ball using the classic techniques of squish and squash to give the illusion that the ball is being shot into the air with great force, making the rubber band vibrate as the ball bounces.

Create an interactive valentine (see Chapter 14) that your recipient can rearrange to make an original creation. You'll learn how to create movie clips that can be dragged at runtime.

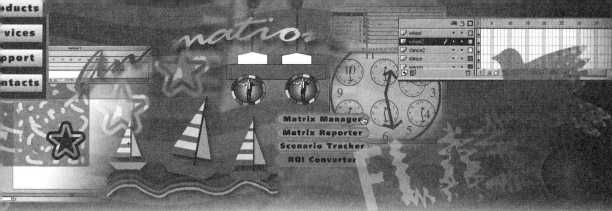

Chapter 11
Basic Animations

Project 1: Create a shape tween

Project 2: Create an animation using onion skin

Project 3: Lock an animation to a motion guide

Project 4: Use *squishing* and *squashing* to create a more realistic animation

By Dan London

Flash and Animation

Flash's animation tools are an easy and powerful way to begin animating. The learning curve is not too steep, and the results are instantaneous. The projects in this chapter are a good place to get your animating feet wet. Who knows, maybe someday you'll be able to convey the aforementioned image on your very own Flash piece.

Project 1: Be There or Be Square

In this example, you'll create a simple shape tween. Shape tweening can be a refreshing alternative to typical motion tweens. Instead of simply fading text in or moving it across the stage, you will change it from one shape into another. In this case you will change squares into the word SQUARE.

1.

Open the Rectangle tool (press R). Change the fill color to the red and black circular gradient. Drag six squares onto the stage and place them in some kind of line near the top of the screen.

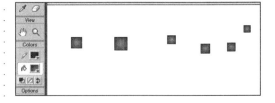

Normally you could drag one instance of a square, turn it into a symbol, and drag out five more instances of it. However, Flash cannot shape tween symbols, so you must create separate art for each tween.

2.

Click Frame 20 and insert a keyframe (press F6 or choose Insert|Keyframe).

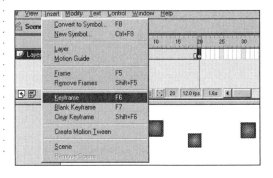

3.

On Frame 20, select all six squares and delete them (Edit|Cut).

Your keyframe bullet will disappear from the Timeline. It will return when you add new content to the frame.

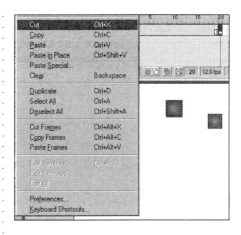

4.

Choose the Text tool (press T). Type "SQUARE". Open the character panel (Window|Panels| Character) and, with the text selected, change the size to 90. Change the text color to blue.

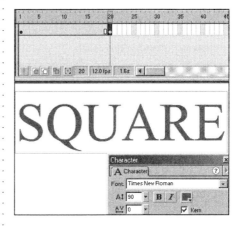

5.

Select the text and choose Modify|Break Apart to break apart the text.

Remember, text cannot be used in a shape tween unless it is broken into a vector graphic or imported as a bitmap.

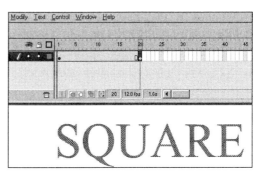

6.

Click Frame 1. Open the Frame panel and choose Shape from the Tweening drop-down menu. Click Play or press Enter to view the tween.

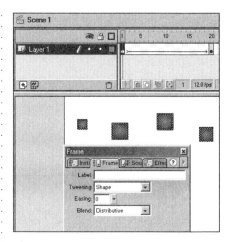

Project 2: Flies Buzzin' 'Round My Head

Though Flash has helpful animation tools to create shape and motion tweens, it is also a traditional frame-by-frame animator. In this example, you will create a very simple animation with the help of onion skinning—a feature that lets you see where your object was placed on a previous frame. Onion skinning lets you animate more complex motions than you have until now with motion tweening.

1.

Open Window|Common Libraries|Graphics. Choose the Mouse graphic and drag it onto the stage. You will use this image as a static graphic for your animation to move around. Name this layer Mouse.

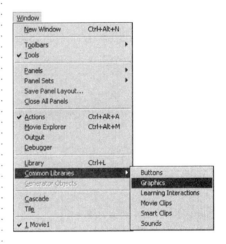

2.

Click Frame 20 and insert a frame (press F5 or Insert|Frame) to make the animation 20 frames long.

3.

Insert a new layer (Insert|Layer) and name it Fly. In the Timeline, drag the Fly layer beneath the Mouse layer.

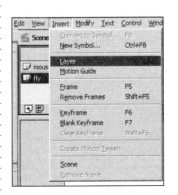

4.

Click Frame 1 of the Fly layer. Activate the Pencil tool and select the Smooth option. Draw a slightly curved line above the right ear of the mouse.

5.

Select Frame 2 of the Fly layer and insert a keyframe onto it (F6 or Insert|Keyframe).

The line you drew in Frame 1 should be highlighted. Press Crtl+X to delete this line from Frame 2. Now, turn onion skinning on. For this example, you will use Onion Skin Outlines.

6.

Though you deleted the drawn line from Frame 2, you can still see where it was because of the onion skinning feature.

Draw a line on Frame 2 that extends the line in Frame 1. Start at the edge of the line in Frame 1.

7.

Repeat the previous two steps through Frame 20. Remember, as you insert each new keyframe, delete the line from the previous frame. If you don't, your animation will show the line growing longer instead of a fly moving. The line on the last frame should almost touch the line on Frame 1. You can check this by dragging the Start Onion Skinning point to Frame 1.

Now you have a fluid animation ready for looping.

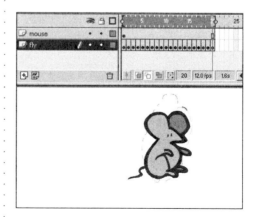

Project 3: Rolling and Tumbling

Sometimes a simple motion tween from Point A to Point B will not do. In those cases, Motion Guide Layers can make the difference between a so-so animation and one that imitates reality, which is what good animation is all about.

For this example, download the rocks.png image from the *Flash 5 Visual Insight* ftp site (**ftp.coriolis.com** in the Public/Flash5VI folder).

1.

Open a new movie and name Layer 1 Rocks. Set the Frame Rate to 15 frames per second. Import rocks.png and place it on the Rocks layer. Drag the image to the bottom of the stage.

2.

Create a new layer and name it Ball. Change the fill color to a gray and white radial gradient. Activate the Oval tool (press O) and drag a circle onto the stage. Select the circle and convert it to a symbol (F8 or Insert|Convert To Symbol). Name the symbol Ball and choose Graphic as its behavior.

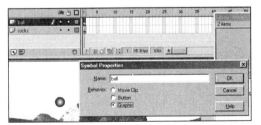

3.

In the Timeline, right-click the Ball layer and choose Add Motion Guide. A new layer called Guide:ball will appear.

4.

Change the stroke color to yellow or any color that will not blend in with the rocks. Activate the Pencil tool and select the Smooth option. Make sure you are on the Guide:ball layer and draw a path on the rocks. Lock the layer.

The path should simulate a ball rolling up to the top of the rocks and rolling down to the bottom.

5.

Select Frame 45 of all three layers, right-click, and choose Insert Frame from the pop-up menu (F5 or Insert|Frame).

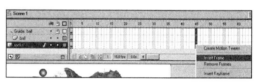

6.

Choose Frame 1 on the Ball layer to select the Ball symbol. Drag the ball onto the top of the Motion Guide until the center snaps to the beginning of the guide.

7.

Now, select Frame 45 of the Ball layer. Choose Insert Keyframe from the pop-up menu (F6 or Insert|Keyframe). Drag the Ball symbol until the center locks to the end of the Motion Guide.

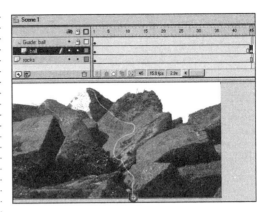

8.

Right-click Frame 1 of the Ball layer and choose Create Motion Tween.

At this point, the ball will roll down the rocks following the guide layer. But you can create a more realistic animation with a few more steps. You will add keyframes and adjust the Ease In/Ease Out value of each tween to add a sense of gravity.

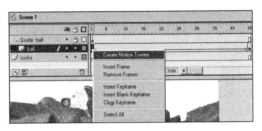

9.

On the Ball layer, insert keyframes each time the ball hits a peak in the rocks. For example, when the ball is at the top of its upward roll, insert a keyframe.

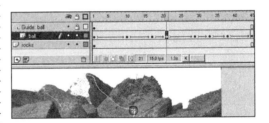

10.

Click Frame 1 of the Ball layer to open the Frame panel. Drag the Easing slider to around -70.

Repeat the step above for the rest of the keyframes.

When the ball travels down the rocks, you want to Ease In the tween. When it rolls up to the peak, you want to Ease Out. Remember, the closer the keyframes are, the closer to 0 the Ease In and Ease Out points should be.

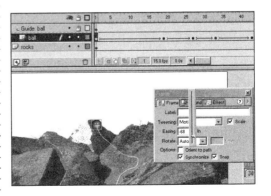

11.

On Frame 1 of the Ball layer, select the Ball symbol. Scale down the ball until it's almost invisible. On each keyframe, gradually increase the ball's height. The best way is to turn on onion skinning and choose Edit Multiple Frames from the options. Be sure to drag your Onion Skin start marker back to the previous keyframe.

Project 4: Spring Has Sprung

In this example, you'll create a version of the classic "bouncing ball" animation. By adding a few extra frames to your animation, you can create a more realistic and professional-looking piece.

1.

Open a new movie with two layers. Name the first layer Ball, and the second layer Sling. The bouncing ball will be placed on the Ball layer; on the Sling layer, you'll create a slingshot to hurl the ball into the air.

2.

First, you will create the sling. Select Frame 1 of the Sling layer. Activate the Line Tool. While pressing Shift, draw a line on the stage. The height should be 0 points and the width 153.6. The line's X and Y coordinates are 79.2 and 186.7, respectively.

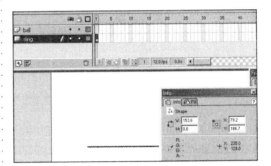

3.

Select Frame 8 of the Sling layer and insert a keyframe. Deselect the line. Bring the cursor toward the bottom of the line. Curve the line so it forms almost a half-circle. The resulting height should be 18.6.

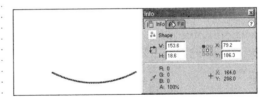

4.

Choose Frame 1 of the Sling layer. Open the Frame panel and create a shape tween.

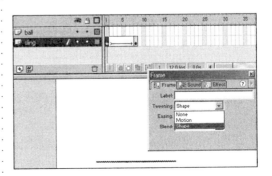

5.

Select and copy Frame 1 of the Sling layer. Paste the frame onto Frame 11. The line now tweens from its original form to a flinging position.

Because you copied a keyframe that was part of a shape tween, the copied frame (Frame 11) will appear in green, signifying that it is also part of the shape tween, if only for one frame. To remove this, click Frame 11 and choose None from the Tweening menu within the Frame's panel.

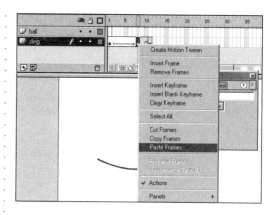

6.

Place the cursor in Frame 8 of the Sling layer and create a shape tween. Frames 12 through 20 will show the flapping of the slingshot (after a slingshot is slung it flaps up and down until it slows to a standstill).

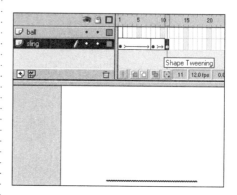

7.

Create a new keyframe on Frame 12 of the Sling layer. Using the Arrow tool, create a slight upward curve in the straight line. The height of this curve should be 8.1.

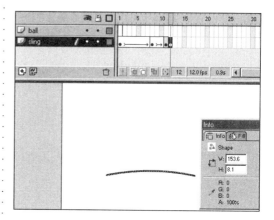

8.

Create a new keyframe on Frame 13 of the Sling layer. Using the Arrow tool, create a slight downward curve in the straight line. The height of this curve should be 7.0.

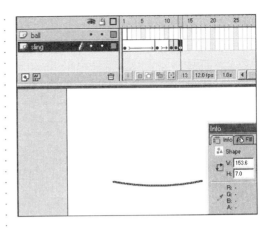

9.

Select Frames 12 and 13 and copy them by right-clicking the two selected frames and choosing Copy Frames from the drop-down menu.

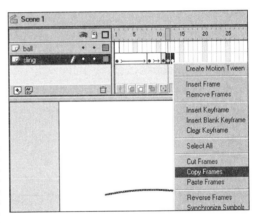

10.

Select Frame 14 and choose Paste Frames. Do this on Frames 16 and 18 as well. You should now have a flapping slingshot.

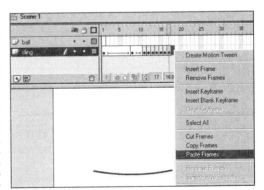

11.

Copy Frame 12 of the Sling layer and paste it onto Frame 20. Adding this frame here starts the slowdown process of the sling on the up-swing and keeps the up-to-down ratio even.

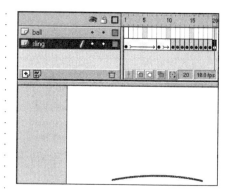

12.

Copy Frame 13 of the Sling layer. Instead of pasting it on the next frame, which would be Frame 21, skip a frame and paste it onto Frame 22. On Frame 20, create a shape tween.

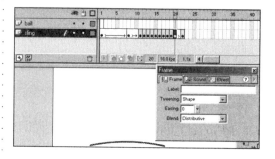

13.

Copy Frame 14 of the Sling layer and paste it onto Frame 24. On Frame 22, create a shape tween.

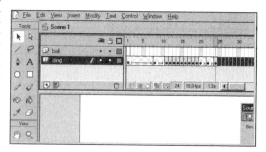

14.

Copy Frame 20 and paste it onto Frame 27. Copy Frame 22 and paste it onto Frame 30. Create a shape tween between Frames 24 and 27 and Frames 27 and 30.

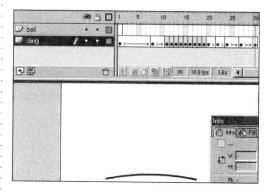

15.

On Frame 30, change the upward curve's height from 8.1 to 4.7.

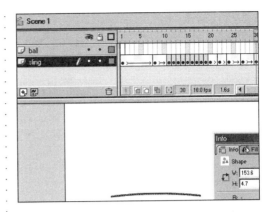

16.

Copy Frame 26 and paste it onto Frame 33. Change the downward curve's height to 2.1. Create a shape tween from Frame 30 to Frame 33.

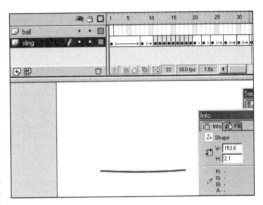

17.

Copy Frame 30 and paste it onto Frame 34. Create a shape tween through Frame 39. You don't need a final keyframe because this animation loops back to Frame 1 to create a fluid movement.

You now have your elastic-like slingshot. Next, you'll create the bouncing ball.

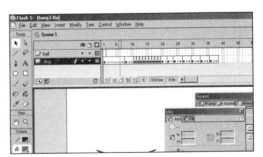

18.

Select Frame 1 of the Ball layer. Click the Marquee tool (press M). Choose the green and black gradient fill and draw a ball (width: 23, height: 23). Place it on the center of your sling (X: 141, Y: 164). Convert the ball to a symbol (F8 or Insert|New Symbol) named Ball with Graphic as its behavior.

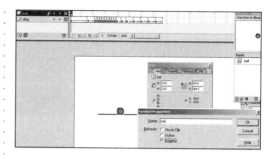

You might wonder why you made the ball a symbol but not the sling: Only symbols can be motion tweened but only non-symbols can be shape tweened.

19.

Insert a keyframe on Frame 8 of the Ball layer. Using the down arrow key on your keyboard, relocate the ball so it sits on top of the sling's downward curve.

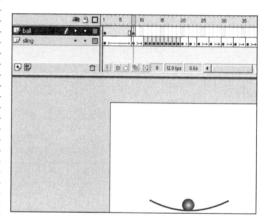

20.

Select Frame 1 of the Ball layer and create a motion tween between Frames 1 and 8.

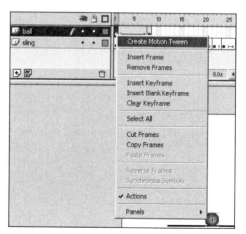

21.

Insert a keyframe on Frame 14 of the Ball layer. Select the Ball symbol. Using the up arrow key on your keyboard, move the ball until it's touching the top of the stage—as if the ball is hitting the ceiling.

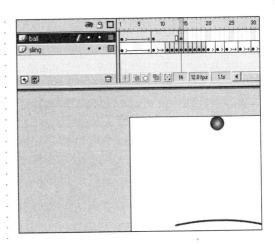

22.

Select Frame 8 of the Ball layer and create a motion tween between Frames 8 and 14.

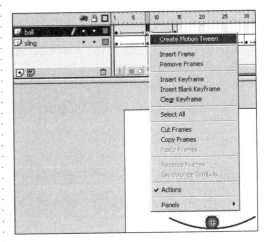

23.

Let's squish the ball a little on its journey toward the ceiling. Select Frame 12 of the Ball layer and insert a keyframe. Select Modify| Transform|Scale and slightly squish the ball to give the appearance of upward resistance.

It's easier to add the squish after you've added the keyframe at the top of the stage. The ball will squeeze in at Frame 12 and squeeze out at Frame 14.

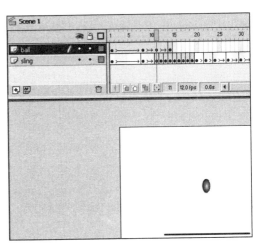

24.

Of course, what would a squish be without a squash? Insert keyframes on Frames 15 and 16 of the Ball layer. On Frame 15, select Modify| Transform|Scale and squash the ball. Make sure you squash it against the ceiling so it appears that smacking against the ceiling caused it to widen slightly. On Frame 16, the ball will snap back to its original shape.

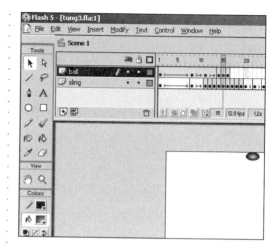

25.

Insert a keyframe on Frame 20 of the Ball layer. Using the down arrow key on your keyboard, move the Ball symbol to the top of the upward curve of the slingshot. Select Frame 16 and create a motion tween.

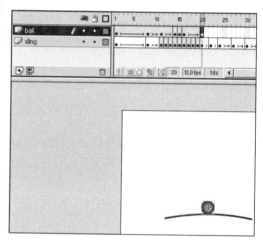

26.

Select Frame 18 of the Ball layer and insert a keyframe. Select Modify|Transform|Scale and slightly squish the ball.

27.

Insert keyframes on Frames 22 and 23. Create a motion tween between Frames 20 and 22. On Frame 22, squash the ball as it smacks against the slingshot.

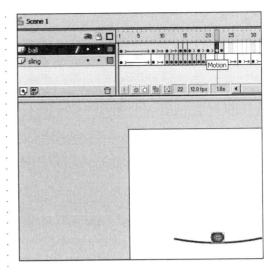

28.

Select Frame 23 and move the ball so that it sits on top of the slingshot.

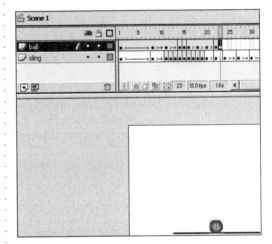

29.

Insert a keyframe on Frame 27 of the Ball layer. Using the up arrow key on your keyboard, move the ball to a little less than halfway to the top of the stage (X: 143, Y: 96). Create a motion tween between Frames 23 and 27.

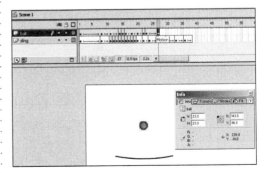

30.

Insert a keyframe on Frame 30. Create a motion tween from Frame 27. Using the down arrow key on your keyboard, move the Ball symbol to the top of the sling.

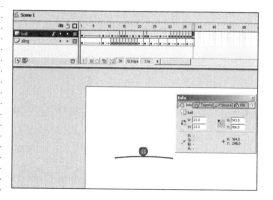

31.

Insert keyframes for Frames 31 through 38. You will do a frame-by-frame animation to simulate a bouncing ball losing momentum. The Y coordinates for the Ball symbol are listed below; the X coordinate is always 143. The key is experimenting to create the most realistic bounce you can.

- *Frame 31—155.7*
- *Frame 32—161.3*
- *Frame 33—155*
- *Frame 34—162*
- *Frame 35—160*
- *Frame 36—156.5*
- *Frame 37—155*
- *Frame 38—156*

32.

Now add some Ease In and Ease Out points to create gravity. Again, experiment with your own settings. Here are the settings I used:

- *Frame 8—Ease out: +47*
- *Frame 16—Ease in: -73*
- *Frame 18—Ease in: -85*
- *Frame 23—Ease out: +38*
- *Frame 27—Ease in: -37*

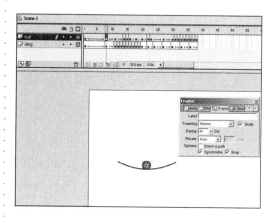

Chapter 12
Using Complex Animations

 Project 1: Create a movie clip and embed it in another one

 Project 2: Create a simple site that uses scenes and loads and unloads a new movie

 Project 3: Use masks to create animated effects

 Project 4: Animate a line of similar objects

By Dan London

Project 1: Everyone's Gone to the Movies

In this example, you will combine two ready-made movie clips into one and animate the new clip. In Flash, you can use many methods to achieve the same results. As you will see from this example, movie clips can be the perfect choice when your project consists of animated loops.

1.

Download the movies.fla file from the Chapter 12 folder on the *Flash 5 Visual Insight* ftp site (**ftp.coriolis.com** in the Public/Flash5VI folder). Open the Library (Cmd/Ctrl+L or Window|Library). The Library should contain three movie clips. You should also see a graphic and two graphic symbols that support the clips.

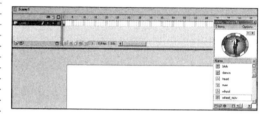

Remember, a movie clip is a portable movie. A symbol needs its supporting graphics to be visible, and a movie clip needs its symbols and the graphics that make up those symbols.

2.

Rename Layer 1 to Dance. From the Library, drag an instance of the Dance movie onto the stage.

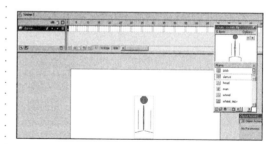

One of the main advantages of a movie clip is that it is independent of the Timeline. You can play this entire clip from within your movie on one frame. Because of this feature, you need to either Publish or Test your movie to view the movie clip doing its thing.

3.

Create a new layer and name it Wheel. Drag an instance of the wheel_mov movie clip onto the stage. Place the wheel_mov clip underneath the Dance clip.

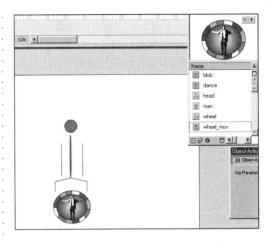

4.

Create a new layer and name it Wagon. With the Rectangle tool, draw a rectangle and place it between the Dance clip and the wheel_mov clip. Select the rectangle and press F8 to turn it into a symbol. Name the symbol Wagon and choose Graphic as its behavior.

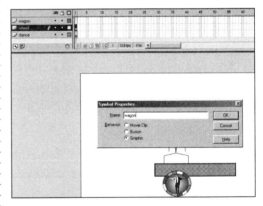

5.

Create a new layer and name it Dance2. Drag another instance of the Dance movie clip to the right of the first dancer. Select it and choose Modify|Transform|Flip Horizontal. You will have one dancer that moves to the left and one that moves to the right.

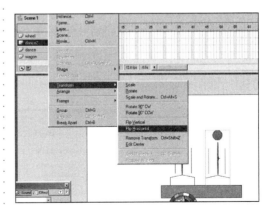

6.

Create a new layer and name it Wheel2. Drag another instance of the wheel_mov movie clip to the right of the first wheel. Arrange the two wheels so that they are even underneath the wagon.

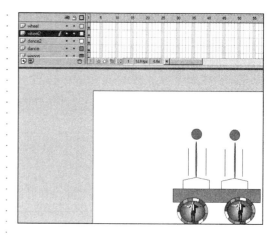

7.

Select all the frames and choose Edit|Copy Frames. Choose Insert|New Symbol. Name the symbol Wagonwheel and choose Movie Clip as its behavior. Inside the symbol window, choose the first frame and paste the frames. Rename the layers to match what resides on them.

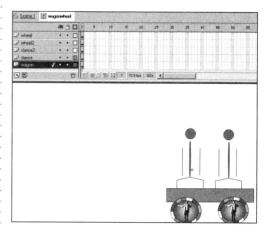

8.

Return to the main Timeline and delete all the layers except for the Wagon layer. You should also delete the wagon itself.

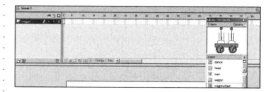

Don't worry about the animation you just created. It is now embedded in the Wagonwheel movie clip.

9.

Drag an instance of the Wagonwheel movie clip onto the stage. Using the Transform tool, scale the clip to about three-quarters of its original size.

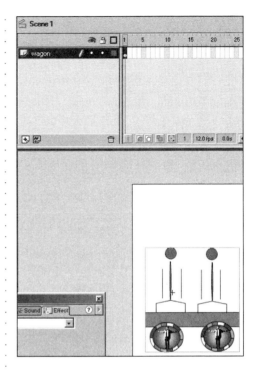

10.

Create a motion guide layer. Draw an upward hilly line. Lock the center of the Wagonwheel clip to the beginning of the motion guide. Add keyframes to Frame 40 of both layers. Lock the Wagonwheel clip to the end of the guide.

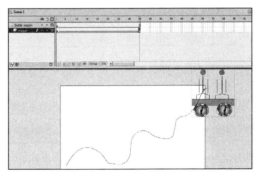

11.

Copy all frames. Open the Blob movie clip and paste the frames on a new layer. Be sure to remove any frames after Frame 40. Rename the layers to match what is on them. Click the Hide Layer tab next to the guide layer to make the guide layer invisible.

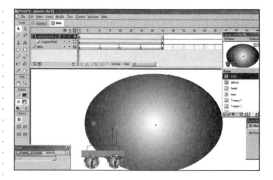

12.

Return to the main stage. Delete all frames and leave one layer. Rename the remaining layer Blob. On Frame 1, drag an instance of the Blob movie clip to the center of the stage.

You now have a one-frame movie that will play a 40-frame movie consisting of three layers that are made up of two other movies that are made up of multiple layers themselves. It's almost like a dream.

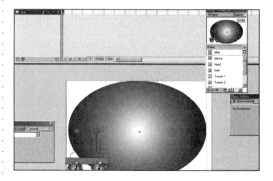

Project 2: You Put the Load Right on Me

In the last example, you embedded one movie *clip* into another. In this example, you will embed an entire *movie* (an .swf file) inside another. You will use one movie to control the other and change the level of control between movies.

1.

Open a new Flash movie. Save it in the same folder at the same level as the .swfs you downloaded for Project 1. Save it as load.fla.

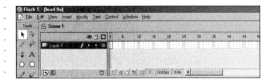

The only way to load an .swf into your current movie is to have that .swf in the same folder on your computer as your current movie. Flash will not accept any path name other than the name of the .swf file itself.

2.

Change the name of Layer 1 to Text. Select Frame 50 and insert a frame there.

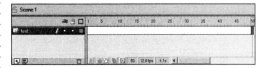

3.

Choose the Text tool. On Frame 1, type the following: "The current movie will load another movie starting at Frame 10. At Frame 40, it will unload the movie. At Frame 50, it will go to Scene2." Drag the text to the bottom of the stage.

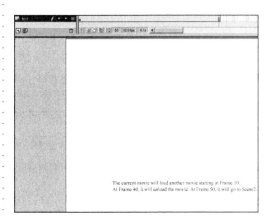

4.

Insert a keyframe at Frame 10. Double-click the frame to bring up the Frame Actions panel. Click Load Movie. Type "welcome.swf" for the URL and choose 1 for Level. Check your work (Control|Test Movie or Cmd/Ctrl+Enter). At Frame 10, a new animation should appear above the text.

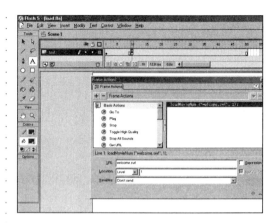

Flash movies work in hierarchies. Level 0 is the parent movie and all others are children. By choosing Level 1, you give your current movie control over the movie you load into it.

5.

Because Flash movies stay in memory even when they aren't visible, it's always good form to unload them once they are done. Doing so reduces the file size of your overall movie.

Insert a keyframe on Frame 40. From the Frame Actions panel, choose Unload Movie. You choose the movie to unload by choosing the level it's on. Choose Level 1.

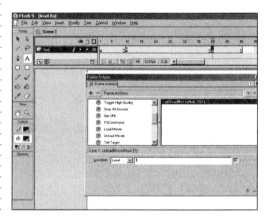

6.

Besides loading and unloading movies, you learn to jump from one scene into another in this example. First, you need to insert a new scene (Insert|Scene). A new blank stage appears. It should be labeled Scene 2.

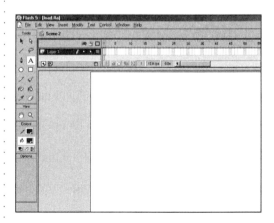

7.

Change the name of Layer 1 to Text. Type the following: "Welcome to Scene 2. At Frame 20, a new movie will be loaded into this scene." Move the text to the top of the stage.

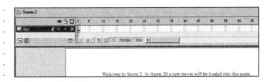

8.

Insert a keyframe on Frame 20 and double-click it. From the Frame Actions panel, choose Load Movie. Type "scene2.swf" as the URL. Choose Level 0. Doing so loads scene2.swf over your current movie—scene2.swf will become the parent movie—and unloads the previous parent from memory.

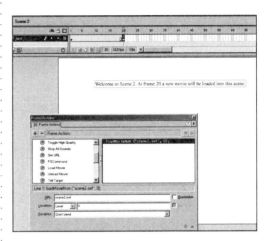

Project 3: Ring Around the Collar

Copying and pasting can be the ultimate timesaver. In this example, you see how you can create an entire piece by creating one layer with animation on it and then copying and pasting that layer.

1.

Open the rings.fla file from the Chapter 12 folder on the ftp site.

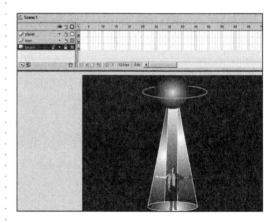

2.

Create a new layer and name it ring_red. Choose red as the stroke color and a transparent fill color. Draw a ring around the top of the beam.

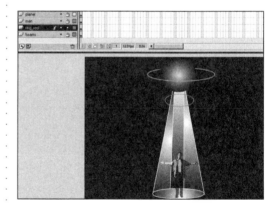

3.

Using the Select tool, select the part of the ring that is on top of the beam and delete it. The ring should now appear to circle the beam.

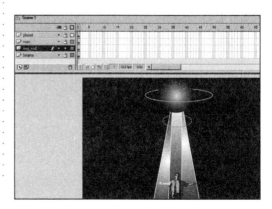

4.

Select Frame 30 of every layer and insert a keyframe (F6 or Insert|Keyframe).

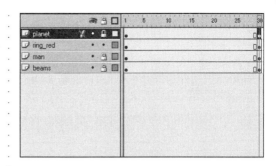

5.

Insert a keyframe on Frame 11 of the ring_red layer. Drag the red ring to the bottom of the beam. Using a scale transform, resize the ring so that it circles the bottom of the beam.

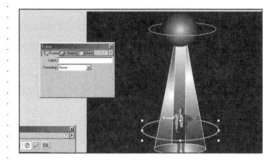

6.

Insert a shape tween between Frames 1 and 11 of the ring_red layer.

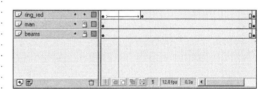

A motion tween creates the same effect (you would have to make the red ring a symbol). However, you will copy and paste the frames you just created, changing the ring colors. If you change a symbol's color, every instance of the symbol changes. Also, because the ring is a small vector animation, copying it without making it a symbol does not significantly increase the file size.

7.

Create a new layer and name it ring_white. Copy Frames 1 through 11 of the ring_red layer. Select Frame 4 of the ring_white layer and paste the frames.

Pasting the frames onto Frame 4 adds five frames to the end of the ring_white layer. Select the handle of the last frame and drag it to Frame 30.

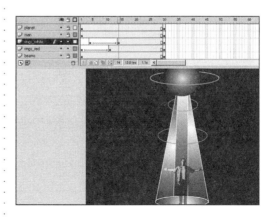

8.

Select Frame 4 of the ring_white layer to select the red ring at the top of the beam. Change the stroke color to white. Select Frame 15 and change this ring to white.

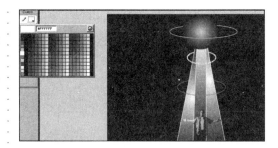

9.

Repeat Steps 7 and 8 every three frames until the last frame of the shape tween is Frame 29.

Create a new layer and paste the frames starting at Frame 10. Remember to change the first and last keyframes of the shape tween and change the colors. Name your layers to correspond to the colors you choose.

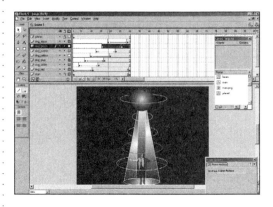

Project 4: Beam Me Up; I've Had Enough

In this project, you learn to use masks. Masks allow you to create unique effects that are original-looking alternatives to the typical motion tween. Even more important, masks give you the power to achieve more realistic animations, such as this example, in which you beam a spotlight from a flying object.

1.

Download beam.fla from the *Flash 5 Visual Insight* ftp site. Open beam.fla and open its Library.

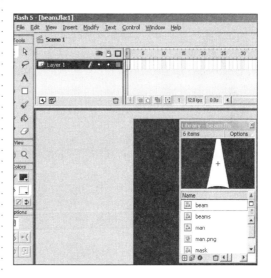

2.

Change the name of Layer 1 to Man. Drag the Man symbol onto the stage and place it so its feet are touching the bottom. In the Effect panel, change the Alpha settings to 60 percent.

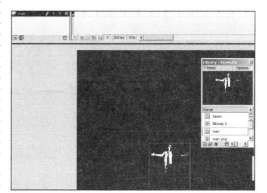

3.

Create a new layer (Insert|Layer) and name it Planet. Drag an instance of the Planet symbol from the Library to the top of the stage. The Planet should be centered above the head of the Man.

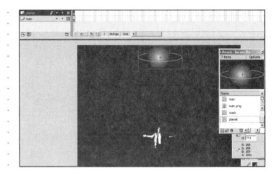

4.

Select the Man layer. Create a new layer and name it Beam. Drag the layer below the Man layer. In the Library, drag an instance of the Beam symbol to the center of the Planet layer.

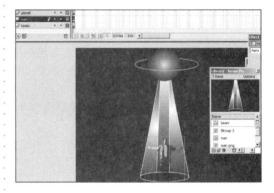

The Beam layer must be below the Man layer and the Planet layer. Changing the Alpha of the Man layer in Step 2 makes it look like the man is standing inside the beam, when the graphic really sits on top. Also, because the Planet layer is the top layer, it looks like the beam is coming from inside the planet.

5.

Create a new layer named Rings. Drag the Rings symbol from the Library and place it above the beam so it appears that the beam is surrounded by the rings.

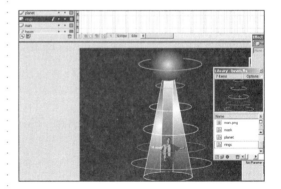

6.

Create a new layer directly above the Beam layer and name it beam_mask. Drag another instance of the Beam symbol onto the stage. Place it directly above the planet so that the bottom of the beam looks as if it's about to swallow up the planet. Right-click the beam_mask layer and choose Mask.

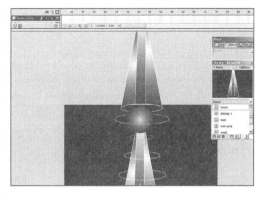

7.

Select Frame 20 of every layer and choose Insert|Keyframe. Activate the beam_mask layer. Be sure to unlock the layer. With Frame 20 selected, drag the instance of the beam so that it sits on top of the original beam. You should not be able to see the beam below the beam mask.

The easiest way to do this is to open the Info panel while the original beam is selected and match the X and Y coordinates to beam_mask.

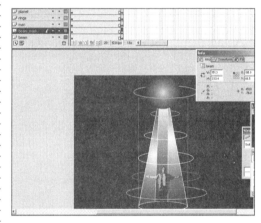

8.

Choose Frame 1 of the beam_mask layer and insert a motion tween (Insert|Create Motion Tween or right-click Frame 1 and choose Create Motion Tween from the drop-down menu) between Frames 1 and 20.

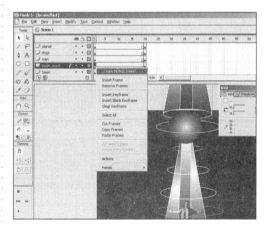

9.

Select Frame 20 of the beam_mask layer and select the Beam symbol. Widen the instance of the Beam symbol (Modify|Transform|Scale) or right-click the instance and choose Scale, so that it completely encompasses the beam below it. Doing this ensures that the entire beam will be visible beneath the mask.

Lock the bottom three layers when you have finished your transform.

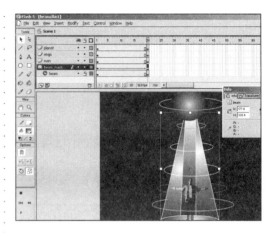

10.

In the Timeline, drag the Man layer directly below the beam_mask layer. The Man layer will now be masked, along with the Beam layer. The animation should now look as if the planet is beaming down onto the man and he is invisible until the light hits him.

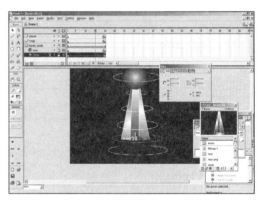

11.

Create a new layer above the Rings layer and name it ring_mask. Right-click the layer and choose Mask. Unlock the layer.

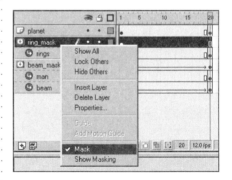

12.

With the Rectangle tool (Press R), draw a rectangle that is wider than the largest ring, which is the last ring from the top. The color of the rectangle doesn't matter because it will be used as a mask.

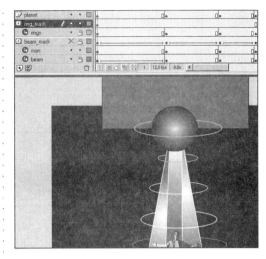

13.

Select the rectangle, which will be used as a mask, and choose Insert|Convert To Symbol (F8). Name the symbol Mask and choose Graphic as its behavior.

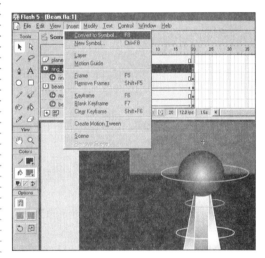

14.

Select Frame 45 of every layer and insert a keyframe (F6 or Insert|Keyframe).

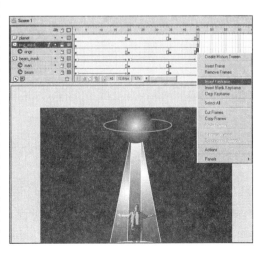

15.

On Frame 20 of the ring_mask layer, insert a keyframe. Select the Mask symbol and scale it so that it masks all the rings. Then choose Frame 1 and create a motion tween between Frames 1 and 20.

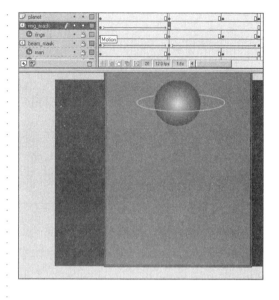

16.

Select Frame 25 of the ring_mask layer and insert a keyframe. Copy Frame 1 and paste it into Frame 25. Create a motion tween between Frames 20 and 25. Insert keyframes on Frames 30, 35, 40, and 45.

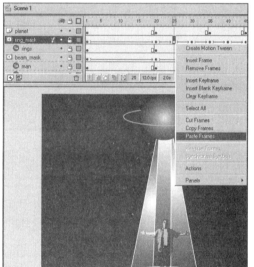

17.

Copy Frame 20 of the ring_mask layer and paste it on Frames 30, 40, and 45.

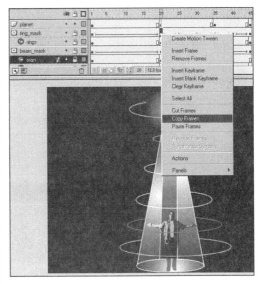

18.

Unlock the Man layer. Make the beam_mask layer invisible so you can see the Man layer. Insert keyframes on Frame 35. On Frame 45, drag the Man symbol into the planet and scale him down until he can't be seen. Insert a motion tween between Frames 35 and 45.

Don't forget to lock all layers and make the beam_mask layer visible at the end of the motion tween. Play your movie.

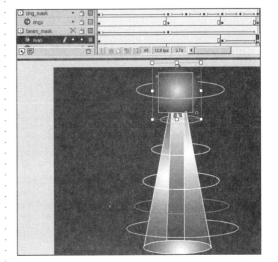

Chapter 13
Using Buttons

Project 1: Create simple navigation buttons with sound

Project 2: Create a drop-down menu

Project 3: Create disjoint rollovers

Project 4: Leave trails as your mouse moves

By Dan London

Project 1: Sound and Vision

In this project, you're going to create a quick Web site for a fictional record company named Flashboy Records. Part of the site has been started for you in files you can find at the *Flash 5 Visual Insight* ftp site (**ftp.coriolis.com** in the Public/ Flash5VI folder). You will be creating navigation buttons and adding sound to the site.

1.

Open Flashboy.fla. Select everything on the SCRAPE layer and press F8 to turn it into a symbol. Name the symbol Scrape and choose Button as its behavior.

2.

Right-click the Scrape button and choose Edit In Place. Insert a keyframe on the Over state in the Timeline. Select the text and change the color to blue. Do the same thing for the Down state, but instead of blue, change the text to red.

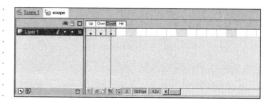

3.

Insert a keyframe for the Hit state. Using the Rectangle tool, draw a box over the entire button.

If you had left the Hit state blank, only the text and the edges would trigger a mouse event, but the inside of the box would not because it is empty. Drawing a box over the button remedies the problem.

4.

Repeat Steps 2 and 3 for the remaining buttons (Lolita and Mao2).

5.

Double-click the Scrape button to open the edit window. Create a new layer and name it Sounds. Insert a keyframe on the Down state of the Sounds layer. Open the Library and drag an instance of the scrape_clip movie clip onto the stage.

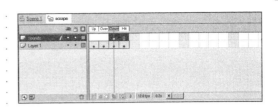

The tunes are movie clips, so they can be associated with Down events on the button without affecting the main Timeline.

6.

Repeat Step 5 for the two remaining buttons and their corresponding tunes (lolita_clip for the Lolita button and mao2_clip for Mao2).

7.

Select Frame 4 of all the layers and insert a frame (F5 or Insert|Frame).

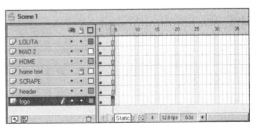

8.

Unlock the home_text layer and insert a keyframe on Frame 2. Select the text and re-place it with the following: "That was a sample of the new hit, "Scrape Tune," by SCRAPE."

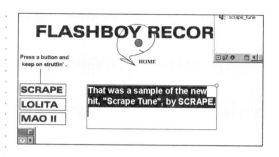

9.

Repeat Step 8 on Frames 3 and 4 of the home_text layer for the other buttons. Be sure to change "SCRAPE" to "LOLITA" on Frame 3 and to "MAO II" on Frame 4.

10.

Select the Scrape button on Frame 1 and open the Object Actions panel. From the Basic Actions menu, choose the Go To action. Type "2" as the Frame and deselect the Go To And Play checkbox. Repeat this step on the two remaining buttons. For Lolita, type "3" as the Frame. For Mao2, type "4".

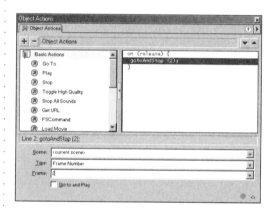

11.

Create a new layer and name it Actions. Double-click Frame 1 to open the Frame Actions panel. Choose the Stop action from the Basic Actions menu.

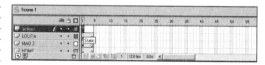

If you skip this step, your movie will play through all four frames, which is not what you want. In this case, you are using the Timeline not for animation, but to separate the pages of your Web site.

12.

Activate the HOME layer and select the HOME text. Press F8 to turn it into a symbol. Name it Home and choose Button as its behavior.

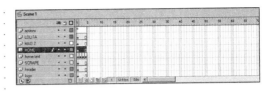

13.

With the Home button still selected, choose the Go To action from the Object Actions panel. Type "1" as the Frame and deselect the Go To And Play checkbox. Select Control|Test Movie and view your project. Click on each button to ensure the flow of the site matches the music behind it.

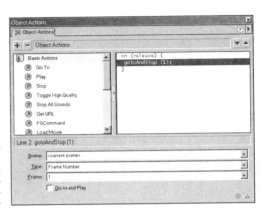

Project 2: On the Menu

In this example, you will use a drop-down menu in place of the sidebar navigation from the previous example.

1.

Open Flashboy_menu.fla from the ftp site. Create a new layer and name it menu_bt. Using the Rectangle tool, draw a rectangle. This shape will become the button that drops down the menu.

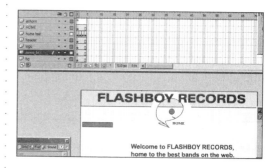

2.

Using the Text tool, type "MENU" and place it on top of the rectangle.

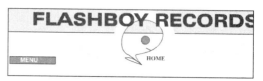

3.

Select the text and the rectangle and convert them into a symbol. Name the symbol menu_bt, and choose Button as its behavior. Drag the newly created button to just under "Flashboy Records".

4.

Create a new layer and name it Menu. Using the Rectangle tool, draw a square large enough to hold the three buttons you created in the previous project. Make sure the width of the square is even with the menu_bt button.

5.

Select the square you just created. Press F8 to convert it into a symbol. Name the symbol menu_drop and choose Graphic as its behavior.

6.

Right-click the menu_drop symbol and choose Edit. From the Library, drag an instance of each of the three buttons you created in the previous project (Scrape, Lolita, and Mao2) onto the square. Arrange them in order and align them flush left.

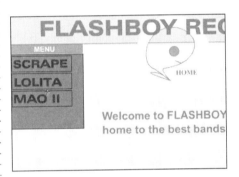

7.

Return to the main stage by selecting Scene 1 above the Timeline. Create a new layer above the Menu layer and name it menu_mask. Draw a square that is the same size as your drop-down menu. Convert it into a symbol named menu_mask. Choose Graphic as its behavior.

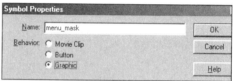

8.

Insert a keyframe on Frame 5 of the menu_mask layer. At Frame 1, while holding the Shift key, drag the mask directly above the menu button. Create a motion tween between Frames 1 and 5. Last, right-click the menu_mask icon in the Timeline and select Mask.

9.

Select the menu_bt button and open the Object Actions panel. From the Basic Actions menu, choose Play. Change the mouse event from Release to Roll Over by deselecting the Release checkbox and checking the Roll Over checkbox.

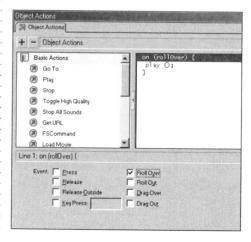

10.

Insert a keyframe at Frame 5 of the Actions layer. Open the Frame Actions panel and choose Stop from the Basic Actions menu.

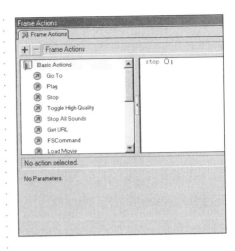

11.

On the menu_mask layer, insert keyframes on Frames 10, 14, 20, 24, 26, and 30. Copy Frame 1 and paste it on Frames 10, 20, and 26. Create motion tweens between Frames 10 and 14, Frames 20 and 24, and Frames 26 and 30.

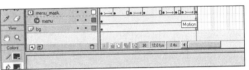

12.

On the Actions layer, copy Frame 1. Paste it onto Frames 10, 14, 20, 24, 26, and 30 to add Stop actions to all these frames.

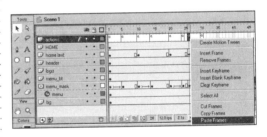

13.

Right-click the menu_drop symbol and choose Edit In Place. Click the Scrape button. From the Object Actions panel, choose the Go To action. Type "10" as the Frame and deselect the Go To And Play checkbox. Do the same thing for the other two buttons, except that the Lolita button goes to Frame 20 and the Mao2 button goes to Frame 26.

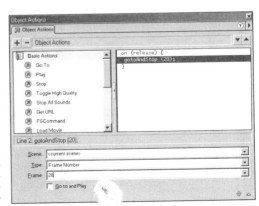

Project 3: The Disjoint Rollover

Buttons can do more than just change colors and play frames. In this example, you will cause a premade movie clip (the bouncing ball from Chapter 11) to play from a rollover button.

1.

Open disjoint.fla from the ftp site. Notice that all it includes is a movie clip named ball.

2.

Change the name of Layer 1 to Button. Using the Oval tool, draw a circle on the stage. The color of the circle is unimportant.

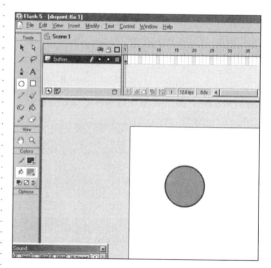

3.

Select the circle and convert it into a symbol (F8). Choose Button as its behavior and name it disjoint_bt.

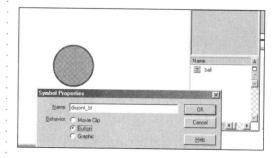

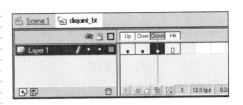

4.

Right-click the disjoint_bt button and choose Edit In Place. Select the color you chose for the inside of the circle. Insert a keyframe (F6) into the Over state. Choose a different color and insert a keyframe (F6) into the Down state. For the Hit state, insert a regular frame (F5).

5.

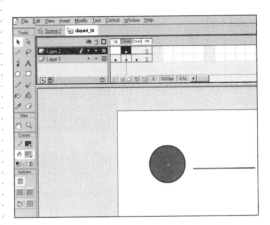

While still in Symbol mode, insert a new layer. Insert a keyframe into the Over state frame. From the Library, drag an instance of the ball movie clip onto the stage.

Return to the main stage and test your movie. When you roll over your button, the bouncing ball movie should play, and when you roll off the button, the movie should cease playing.

Project 4: The Blue Trail

For this project, you will use trail.fla from the ftp site. It contains a premade movie clip that will be triggered by a rollover mouse event.

1.

Open trail.fla from the ftp site. Choose Insert|New Symbol. Name the symbol Trigger and select Button as its behavior.

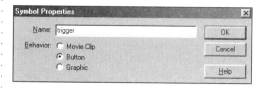

2.

In the Edit Symbol mode, insert a keyframe (F6) and drag an instance of the "flash" movie clip from the Library.

Leave the Up state blank to create a "landmine" effect: Your button still functions like a button, yet it is invisible to users until they trigger it by rolling over it with the mouse.

If Flash inserts the keyframe into the Up state, just drag the keyframe onto the frame for the Over state and remove any other frames that were added.

3.

Insert a blank keyframe (F7) in the Down state and a keyframe (F6) in the Hit state. With the Hit frame selected, draw a circle. Remember that the Hit state can affect a bigger or smaller area than the button itself.

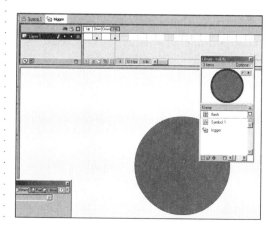

4.

Return to the main Timeline by selecting the Scene 1 tab above the Timeline. Drag an instance of the Trigger button onto the stage.

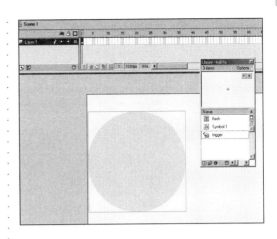

5.

Drag more instances of the Trigger button to fill the entire stage.

6.

You are now ready to test your movie (Control|Test Movie or Cmd/Crtl+Enter). Notice how the movie clip plays as your mouse triggers each button. Because the hit states are so large and the buttons are placed over the entire stage, it appears that the clip is following your cursor.

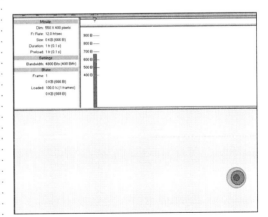

Chapter 14
Creating and Using Forms

Project 1: Create a tip calculator

Project 2: Use forms to validate user information

Project 3: Create an interactive Valentine's Day card

By Dan London and
Sherry London

Putting Forms to Work

You can use forms to ascertain information about users. Forms can also be thought of as mini-applications. In this Project chapter, you will create the beginnings of a tip calculator, validate user information, and create an interactive Valentine's Day card.

Project 1: Tip Me with Your Best Shot

In this example, you will create a tip calculator. It will classify three types of tips: bad service, which will get a 10 percent tip; average service, which will get 15 percent; and above-average service, which will get 20 percent.

1.

Select the Text tool and type "Price of Dinner" onto the stage.

2.

In the Text Options panel, select Input Text in the top drop-down menu and Single Line in the second drop-down menu. Type "dinner" inside the Variable text box. Make sure the Border/Bg checkbox is checked. Type "12" for Max Characters; this value sets the maximum number of characters that the text box accepts.

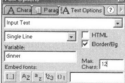

3.

Type "Tip =" to the right of the text box.

4.

Using the Text tool, click a space to the right of the Tip = text. In the Text Options panel, select Dynamic Text from the drop-down menu. For the Variable name, type "tip." This time, deselect the Border/Bg checkbox. The result of the tip calculation will appear here.

5.

Create a button and place it on the stage. Beneath this button, type "Below average service".

6.

Copy the button and paste it twice onto the stage. Below the first copy, type "Average Service", and below the second one, type "Good Service".

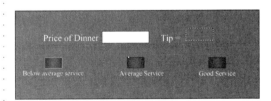

7.

Select the first button and open the Object Actions panel. From the Actions menu, double-click Set Variable. In the Variable text box, type "tip". In the Value text box, type "dinner * .10". Make sure the Expression checkbox associated with the Value box is checked.

The variable Tip refers to the text box named Tip, which is where the tip will appear. The variable Dinner is the number the user will enter.

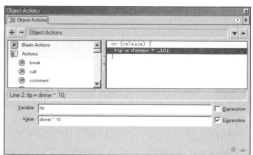

8.

Repeat the above step for the remaining two buttons. For the Average Service button, the Value should be "dinner *.15." For the Good Service button, the value should be "dinner *.20" for the good tippers inside us all.

You can add a number of features to this script, such as handling decimal points and rounding up the results. ActionScript can handle these refinements, but they are beyond the scope of this book, and will not be covered here.

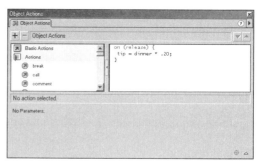

Project 2: Constant Validation

In the following example, you will create a form with three fields. Each field will be validated to ensure something is entered in the text box. Once the form has been filled out correctly, the results will be printed on the screen.

1.

Create three Input Text boxes with borders and place them on the stage as in the figure. Their Variable names should be lname, fname, and email.

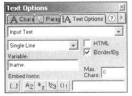

2.

To the left of the lname input box, type "Last Name". For fname, type "First Name", and for email, type "Email".

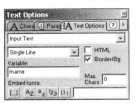

3.

Open the Common Library and drag an instance of a button onto the stage. (I chose the Pill button). Scale the button down to a reasonable size.

4.

Above the button, type "Submit".

5.

On Layer 1 add keyframes to Frames 1 through 8. Add a Stop action on Frame 1.

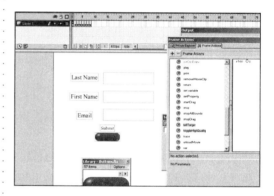

6.

Select the Submit button and, from the Object Actions panel, add a Go To And Stop action on Frame 2.

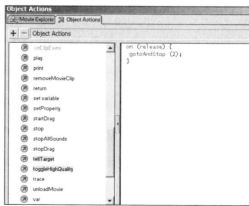

7.

Frames 3, 5, and 7 will be message frames. Select Frame 3 and type "PLEASE TYPE YOUR LAST NAME" at the top of the stage. Select Frame 5 and type "PLEASE TYPE YOUR FIRST NAME". Select Frame 7 and type "PLEASE TYPE YOUR EMAIL ADDRESS".

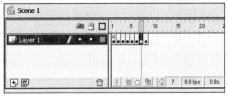

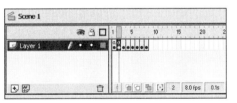

8.

Select Frame 2 and type the following code into the Frame Actions panel:

```
if (lname eq "") {
    gotoAndStop (3);
} else {
    gotoAndStop (4);
}
```

The code says that if the Input Box with the Variable name lname is blank, then Go To And Stop at Frame 3, which is the message frame. But if something is written in the Input Box, continue to Frame 4.

9.

Now write the same code for Frames 4 and 6, changing the variables to the appropriate names and the Go To And Stop frames to the appropriate frames.

For Frame 4, type this code:

```
if (fname eq "") {
    gotoAndStop (5);
} else {
    gotoAndStop (6);
}
```

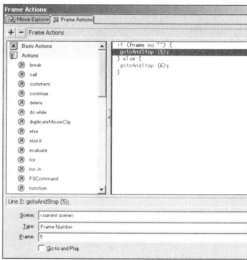

10.

For Frame 6, type the following code:

```
if (email eq "") {
    gotoAndStop (7);
} else {
    gotoAndStop (8);
}
```

ActionScript can also detect whether the email address entered is valid by checking for characters like the "." in the address or an @ sign, but this type of scripting is beyond the scope of this example.

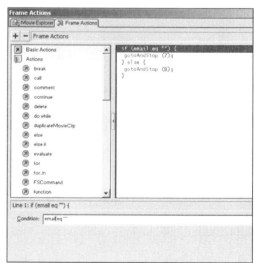

11.

Select Frame 8 in the Timeline (all the objects should be selected). Select Cut from the Edit menu. Now type the following three lines:

```
Your last name is
Your first name is
Your email address is
```

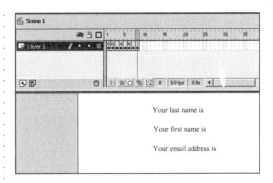

12.

Place a Dynamic Text box next to each line of type. Uncheck the Border/Bg and Selectable checkboxes. Type "last" as the Variable name for the box next to the *Your last name is* line. Type "first" as the Variable name for the *Your first name is* line. Type "mail" as the Variable name for the *Your email address is* line. Make the text box for the email larger than the other text boxes so it can accommodate a long email address.

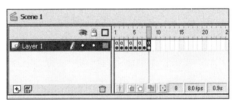

13.

You will set three Variables by using ActionScript code in the Frame Actions panel. The Variables will be the names of the dynamic text boxes on this frame. The Value will be the names of the previous input boxes. Select the Expression option for each Variable; this will tell Flash to grab the information out of the input boxes and display that information in these dynamic text boxes.

The code should look like the following:

```
last = lname;
first = fname;
mail = email;
```

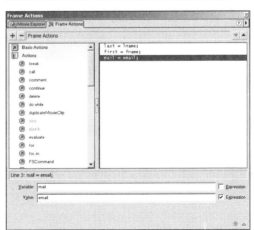

Project 3: Be My Valentine

A form does not have to consist of input fields and checkboxes; it can also be an interactive area for freeform play. In this example, you'll create an interactive greeting card, similar to those on many of the free greeting card Web sites. You'll need to download the valentine.fla file from the *Flash 5 Visual Insight* ftp site (**ftp.coriolis.com** in the Public/Flash5VI folder).

1.

Open valentine.fla. You'll see Scene 1. (The file contains three scenes.)

2.

Open Scene 3. This is the scene to which you'll add interactivity. You'll convert many of the objects in this scene to button symbols and add startDrag and stopDrag commands to them.

3.

Double-click the symbol BE to edit it in place.

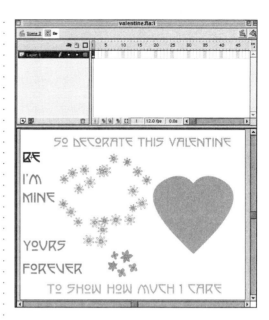

4.

Choose Insert|Convert To Symbol (F8).

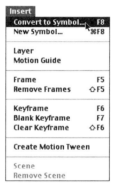

5.

In the Symbol Properties dialog box, name the symbol BeButton and set the Behavior to Button.

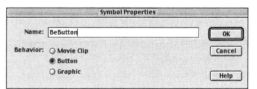

6.

Double-click the new BeButton symbol and open the button Timeline. Move the playhead to the Hit state and press F6 to add a keyframe.

If you leave the Hit state covering the same area as the text, your users will have a hard time moving the text to decorate the heart.

7.

Select the Rectangle tool. Make the Fill color Black and set the Stroke color to None. Create a rectangle that covers the text on the Hit state.

8.

Click the Be symbol at the top of the Timeline to return the movie to the Timeline for the symbol Be.

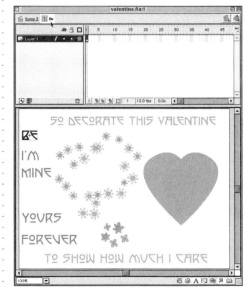

9.

Select the symbol (you're selecting the BeButton symbol that's placed inside the Be symbol). In the Object Actions panel, open the Basic Actions section and double-click the startDrag command.

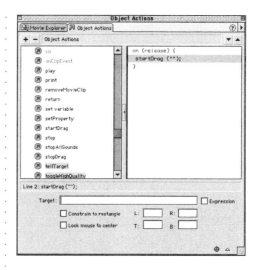

10.

Highlight the On Release line in the right pane of the Object Actions panel. Change the Button Event to On Press by deselecting the Release checkbox and selecting the Press checkbox.

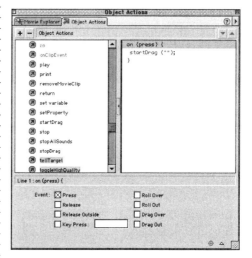

11.

Highlight the last line of the ActionScript code and double-click the stopDrag command.

12.

Click Scene 3 at the top of the Timeline to re-turn to the main Timeline.

13.

Repeat Steps 3 through 12 for the following elements:

- I'm (becomes Ibutton)
- Mine (becomes Minebutton)
- Yours (becomes Yoursbutton)
- Forever (becomes Foreverbutton)

Remember to create Hit states for the text.

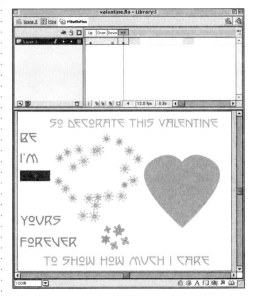

14.

Repeat Steps 3 through 5 and 9 through 12 for the following elements that don't need special Hit states:

- Flowers (becomes Flowersbutton)
- Violets (becomes Violetsbutton)
- Heart (becomes Heartbutton)

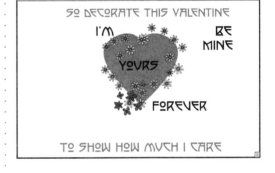

15.

Choose Control|Test Movie to play the movie. Click the Continue button to move from Scene 1 to Scene 2 to Scene 3. In Scene 3, click and drag the various objects around to decorate the heart.

16.

As an added challenge, you can add an instance of the Continue button to the page so that you can go to the beginning of the movie to start over.

Chapter 15
Producing Flash Movies

Project 1: Create a simple Preloader

Project 2: Create a slide show with Bandwidth Profiling

Project 3: Export a complete site

By Matthew David

Project 1: Create a Simple Preloader

Flash movies have become famous for being compact and light in file size. With that said, it is amazing how large those compact files can get when audio and a lot of imported graphics are packed into them. The following project demonstrates how to add a simple preloading animation; the Preloader plays an animation to let the user know that the rest of the movie is downloading.

1.

Begin by opening the file simple_preloader.fla from the *Flash 5 Visual Insight* ftp site (**ftp.coriolis.com** in the Public/Flash5VI folder). The movie opens with a default of one scene. Add a second scene by selecting Insert|Scene.

2.

The Preloader will be placed into Scene 1. Before we do this let's add some content to Scene 2. Open Scene 2. Add one layer; name the first layer Scripts and the second layer Content. Make each layer five frames long. Additional frames can be inserted with the F8 key.

3.

Select the Content layer and type the following text: "This is Scene 2".

In a production Flash movie, you would place the main movie in this section.

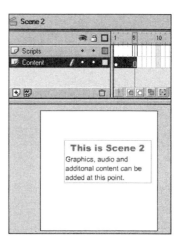

4.

Select the Scripts layer. Choose Frame 5 and open the Frame Actions panel. From Basic Actions double-click Stop to add it to the ActionScript editor window.

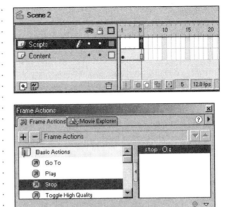

5.

Open Scene 1. Rename Layer 1 as Preload. Make the Preload layer five frames long. Change each frame into a keyframe (F6).

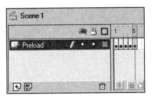

6.

Select Frame 1. Using the Text tool type "Loading" in the center of the stage. Make the font Arial Black (or Helvetica) and the size 12 points. Set Paragraph to left align.

7.

Copy the word "Loading" from Frame 1 and paste it into Frames 2 through 5. The word should be in the same place for each frame (you can quickly accomplish this using Edit|Paste In Place). Select Frame 2. Select the word "Loading" and double-click it to open it in edit mode. Add a single period immediately after the word.

8.

Select Frame 3 and edit the word "Loading" by adding two periods after the word. Add three periods after the word on Frame 4 and four periods on Frame 5.

9.

Select Frame 1 and open the Frame Actions panel. From Basic Actions select If Frame Is Loaded. Set the options as follows: Scene: Scene 2; Type: Frame Number; Frame: 5. The script will tell Flash that it must preload all of the content up to Frame 5 of Scene 2.

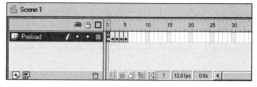

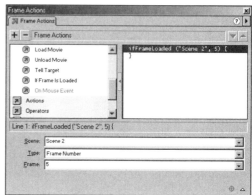

10.

Double-click the Go To action. Set the options to Scene 2, Frame Number, and 1. Make sure the Go To And Play option is checked. The script tells Flash what to do when all of the frames of Scene 2 are loaded. In this case, the movie automatically goes to Frame 1 of Scene 2 and begins playing.

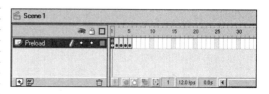

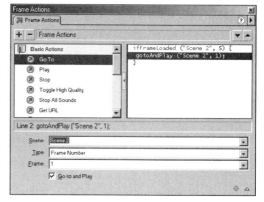

11.

Choose Frame 5. In the Frame Actions panel, double-click the Go To action. Set the options as Scene 1, Frame Number, and 1. The script will cause the animation to keep repeating until all of the content in Scene 2 is loaded.

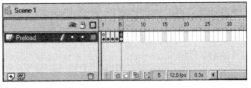

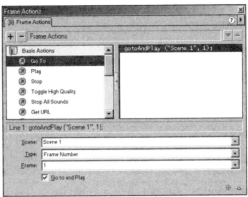

12.

The movie can now be tested. Press F12 to preview the movie in your Web browser. You will notice that while Scene 2 is loading the "Loading…" animation will keep playing. The more content in Scene 2, the longer the preload scene will remain up. When uploaded to a Web server and viewed over the Internet, the Preloader's purpose becomes apparent. Preloading allows you to create movies that have the same impact on a customer whether they are accessing the Internet on a dial-up modem or a dedicated high-speed connection.

Loading.	Loading..	Loading...
Loading....	Loading.....	Loading.

Project 2: Create a Slide Show with Bandwidth Profiling

While a Flash movie is playing, there will be instances when only a few graphics appear and other times when a lot of graphics and sound files play simultaneously. These situations create *peaks* and *troughs* in the presentation of the movie. Slower Internet connections may not be able to play back the animation at the original intended speed due to these peaks. To combat this, Flash provides a Bandwidth Profiler that shows you how the movie is peaking. The following project demonstrates how the Profiler can be used to enhance your movie's playback to take the presentation of the movie to the next level of customer satisfaction.

1.

Open the movie bandwidthprofiling.fla from the *Flash 5 Visual Insight* ftp site. The movie is composed of one layer with four frames; each frame is a keyframe. Each frame contains a picture, and each picture is a button. These four frames will represent a simple presentation. The images must be clicked with the mouse to move from one frame to the next.

2.

Select Frame 1. Open the Frame Actions panel and double-click the Stop action from Basic Actions.

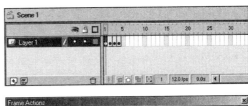

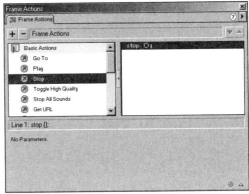

3.

Choose the image in Frame 1. In the Object Actions panel, double-click the On Mouse Event action. Change the settings to Press and Release.

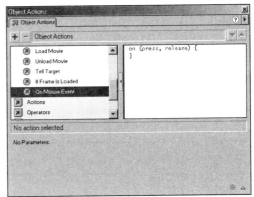

4.

In the Object Actions panel, double-click the Go To option. Set the options as follows: Scene: <current scene>; Type: Frame Number; Frame: 2. Make sure to uncheck the Go To And Play option.

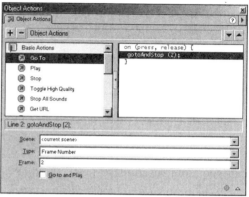

5.

Repeat Steps 3 and 4 for Frames 2 and 3. Change the number of the Go To action to Frames 3 and 4, respectively.

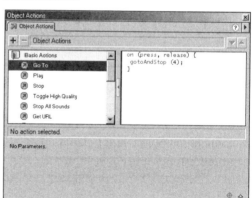

6.

For the Go To event on Frame 4 change the frame number to 1. The movie can now be previewed. Clicking on each image will navigate the customer through the movie one frame at a time. When the customer gets to the last frame they are sent back to Frame 1.

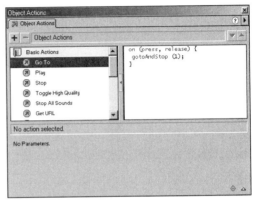

7.

Preview the movie by selecting Ctrl+Enter. The movie will preview within Flash. Open the Bandwidth Profiler from View|Bandwidth Profiler. The Profiler provides information on how your movie will download over the Internet. We see that the current movie is four frames in length, the SWF file size is 13KB, and the file will take 5.4 seconds to preload. Each of the images used in the movie shows up on the Profiler as a peak. Larger graphics will show up as taller peaks. Each graphic can be selected to view individual statistics, such as download time.

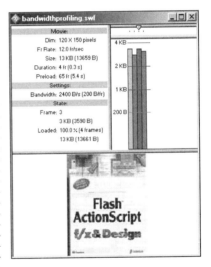

8.

You can simulate the loading of the movie in Flash. From the View menu select Show Streaming. The movie immediately begins to play at a simulated Internet connection speed. The default setting emulates a 28.8Kbps modem.

9.

Select Debug from the top menu bar to open a list of connection speeds to simulate how a movie will download over the Internet. Next to each connection speed is a download speed. This number represents a "fair" download speed typically experienced by users connecting to the Internet.

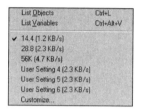

10.

The settings for the Internet connections can be modified. Select Debug|Customize to open the Custom Modem Settings window. Change User Setting 4 to ISDN. Change the Bit Rate to 128000 to represent the connection speed of an ISDN user over the Internet.

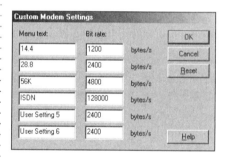

11.

Select Debug and change the default settings to ISDN. The Bandwidth Profiler now changes the statistics of the movie to reflect the movie being downloaded over an ISDN Internet connection. Use the Bandwidth Profiler to locate peaks of movies and to examine how a movie will be downloaded over different Internet connection speeds.

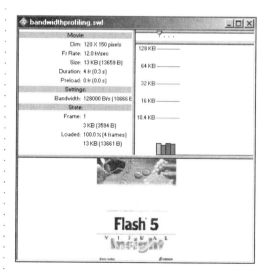

Project 3: Exporting a Complete Site

The final step for any Flash movie is the export process. The export process converts the Flash FLA file format into one that can be read in a Web browser supporting the Flash Player. This is called *shocking* a movie. The following project demonstrates how a movie can be shocked with customized settings.

1.

Open the movie exportsettings.fla from the *Flash 5 Visual Insight* ftp site. The movie is a simple animation of a bouncing ball.

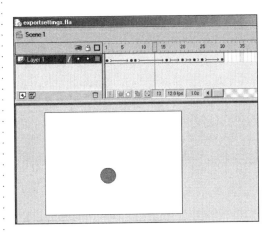

2.

The movie must be optimized for delivery over the Internet. Select File|Publish Settings to reveal the settings needed to do this.

3.

The Publish Settings window shows the 10 different formats in which a Flash movie can be exported. For delivery over the Internet through a Web browser, choose the settings Flash (.swf) and HTML (.html). This will create both a SWF movie file and a HTML container file (with OBJECT and EMBED tags).

4.

Select the Flash tab in the Publish Settings window. The default format is to load the movie Bottom Up. This can be changed to Top Down. The customer downloading the movie will see almost no difference between the two formats.

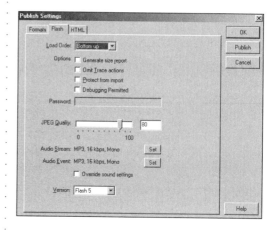

5.

Security is an important issue on the Internet. The default SWF file format cannot be modified once it is created. However, this does not stop illegal use of a movie created through the Load Movie action. Select Protect From Import under Options to prevent this. You can now add a password. Type in the password "Flash_password". (All passwords are case sensitive.) For extra security, use passwords with a combination of lower- and uppercase letters and numbers.

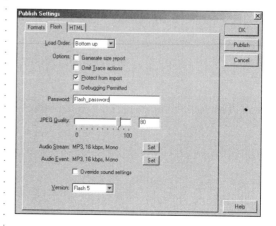

6.

All raster images imported into a Flash movie are exported as JPEG graphics. JPEG Quality is set to 80 by default, which is a good level to start with. For greater clarity, drag the slider towards 100. The higher the JPEG level, the longer the JPEG graphics will take to download. Use the Bandwidth Profiler to see how much longer a movie will take to download with larger JPEGs.

7.

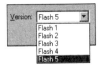

In Flash 5, the default SWF version setting is for Flash 5 movies. This version will allow any of the latest Flash extensions to be used. However, using SWF will also require that your user has installed the Flash 5 Player. For simple animations, such as the bouncing ball, Flash versions 1 through 3 should be used. The older the player, the greater the chance the user coming to your site can successfully view the movie. It must be noted, however, that using an old Flash format may result in reanimating or re-scripting a movie, particularly if masks or any ActionScript were used.

8.

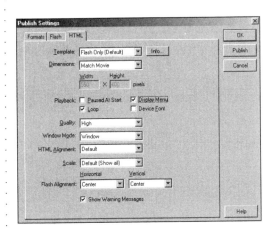

Select the HTML tab. For our animation the movie Template setting is Flash Only (Default). The dimensions of the movie are Match Movie.

9.

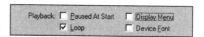

Playback allows for HTML settings that will trigger the movie to continuously loop. Deselect Display Menu. This action will prevent a user from right-clicking a Flash movie and displaying the Flash Player menu. Select OK to save the settings.

10.

Save the movie of the bouncing ball to a folder. Now select File|Publish. You will now find exportsettings.fla in the same folder with exportsettings.swf and exportsettings.htm. Double-click exportsettings.htm to view the Flash movie in your Web browser.

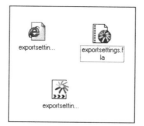

Index

If you *like* this book, you'll *love...*

Illustrator® 9 Visual Insight
by T. Michael Clark
248 pages

ISBN #: 1-56710-749-3
$24.99 (US) $37.99 (CAN)

Illustrator® 9 Visual Insight helps you quickly grasp this powerful illustration software to create eye-catching images. Learn Illustrator's basic features—drawing techniques; using layers, masks, filters, and actions; and creating illustrations for the Web. Then, the step-by-step projects help you to develop your own powerful artwork. You will learn to produce brochures, scanned line art, Web interfaces, and much more!

Dreamweaver™ 4 Visual Insight
by Greg Holden and Scott Wills
336 pages

ISBN #: 1-57610-924-0
$24.99 (US) $37.99 (CAN)

Through illustrations and screen shots, *Dreamweaver™ 4 Visual Insight* will lead beginners through a tour of Dreamweaver's most important tools and functions. Readers will learn how to convert text files to Web pages, add/edit Web pages images, make global changes to Web sites, and publish a Web site. This book provides an easy and practical starter guide for professional designers who are new to the Internet, as well as technical novices who need a user-friendly yet powerful application for designing and managing fully functional Web sites.

Flash™ 5 f/x and Design
by Bill Sanders
384 pages with CD-ROM

ISBN #: 1-57610-816-3
$49.99 (US) $74.99 (CAN)

Beginning with the core concepts and tools of Flash™ 5, *Flash 5 f/x and Design* explores ways to create attractively effective Flash movies. This book is not an art or design lesson, but rather it shows the reader how to use Flash 5 tools to create lively animations and designs using one's own artistic talents, tastes, and imagination. It covers the basics but also goes beyond into a solid introduction of ActionScript, adding Flash 5 animation to QuickTime Movies, and even importing external data. Each Flash 5 element is supported by step-by-step examples and projects guiding the reader through the details of Flash 5's powerful set of possibilities. The accompanying CD-ROM contains 50 projects in both FLA and SWF files, allowing readers to see the finished results plus examine the projects and examples in the book to better understand how to apply the techniques to one's own work. Attention to detail such as mixing color schemes, crucial ActionScripting, using the new panels for precision placement and scaling, plus other Flash 5 innovations make this title a must-have book for the Flash designer and developer.

GoLive™ f/x and Design
by Richard Schrand
480 pages with CD-ROM

ISBN#: 1-57610-786-8
$49.99 (US) $74.99 (CAN)

From basic designs to advanced rollover techniques, *GoLive™ 5 f/x and Design* takes you on a tour of the hottest features of this high-end Web design program. Learn about Cascading Style Sheets, get ideas on how to create eye-catching forms, find out how to build dynamic sites by using today's cutting-edge technology, and then discover how the author builds an entire site using the techniques discussed throughout the book. The accompanying CD-ROM includes tutorials, background art, as well as trial and shareware programs that help and inspire readers to create exciting sites.

Flash forward with Coriolis book

Flash™ ActionScript f/x and Design

by Bill Sanders

ISBN #: 1-56710-821-X
$44.99 (US) $67.99 (CAN)
344 pages with CD-ROM

Using ActionScript, the Flash™ 5 developer can add interactive functionality like never before—a quantum leap from previous versions of this scripting language for Flash! Through numerous projects and examples, *Flash™ ActionScript f/x and Design* explains how to get the most out of Flash 5 using Action-Script, including the actions (statements), operators (with significant changes from previous versions), functions (including user functions), properties, and the many new objects and their methods. This book leads the reader through all the elements of the new ActionScript, and an Example Glossary provides a quick lookup with a sample script for all of the many actions, operators, functions, and properties. The book's CD-ROM includes the source files (FLA) and the SWF files so the reader can examine and run the coding for all the projects. Flash™ 5 trial software is also included.

Flash™ 5 Visual Insight

by Sherry London and Dan London

ISBN #: 1-57610-700-0
$24.99 (US) $37.99 (CAN)
384 pages

Flash™ 5 Visual Insight provides an illustrative, simple approach to this leading Web-development program. The format grabs the readers' attention with screenshots and caption-like text teaching the applicable and useful fundamental elements of this program, such as tools and their options. Building on that base, projects then guide readers through creating their own exciting movies!

Flash™ 5 f/x and Design

by Bill Sanders

ISBN #: 1-57610-816-3
$49.99 (US) $74.99 (CAN)
416 pages with CD-ROM

Beginning with the core concepts and tools of Flash™ 5, this book shows the reader how to use Flash 5 tools to create lively animations and designs using one's own artistic talents, tastes, and imagination. *Flash™ 5 f/x and Design* goes beyond the basics into a solid introduction of ActionScript like adding Flash animation to QuickTime Movies, and even importing external data. Step-by-step projects and examples familiarize the reader with Flash 5's powerful possibilities. The accompanying CD-ROM contains 50 projects in both FLA and SWF files, allowing readers to examine the projects and examples from the book in order to understand how to apply the techniques to one's own work. Detail such as mixing color schemes, crucial ActionScripting, using the new panels for precision placement and scaling, plus other Flash 5 innovations make this title a must-have book for the Flash designer and developer.

Flash™ 5 Cartoons an Games f/x and Desi

by Bill Turner,
James Robertson,
and Richard Bazley

ISBN#: 1-57610-958-5
$49.99 (US) $74.99 (CA
350 pages with CD-ROM

This book covers Flash™ from a cartoon and gami aspect. Learn how to cohesively pull together c create all the necessary elements for an entertain cartoon show. Create car characters for television c music videos; then, disco how to use those cartoon elements when scripting programming interactive games on the Internet. T book includes a CD-ROM a complete full-length ca show and source codes fc several games. With Flas Cartoons and Games f/x a Design, you will go beyor the general description o the various Flash tools a discover what can be do with them!